PHANTOM LETTERS

A War Story... A Love Story

PHANTOM LETTERS

A War Story... A Love Story

GARY K. THRASHER

Langdon Street Press
Minneapolis, MN

Langdon Street Press
212 3rd Avenue North, Suite 290
Minneapolis, MN 55401
612.455.2293
www.langdonstreetpress.com

ISBN-13: 978-1-936183-52-4
LCCN: 2010939172

Cover Design and Typeset by Melanie Shellito

Printed in the United States of America

Fred.

Thanks for serving your uncle Sam.

This is one year of my service — Carole served at home, but served all the same.

All the best,

GK Thrasher

TABLE OF CONTENTS

DEDICATION

For Bruce Ducat and Gene Knudsen, who gave their lives for their country, and all my comrades in the 389th tactical fighter squadron who fought the air war in Vietnam. They were the last of a breed: fighter pilots who fought the old fashioned way—close to the ground. This is their story, too.

FOREWORD

The Combat Aviator

Say what you will about him: Arrogant, cocky, boisterous, and a fun-loving fool to boot. He has earned his place in the sun. Across the span of ninety years he has given this country some of its proudest moments and most cherished military traditions. But fame is short-lived and little the world remembers. Almost forgotten are the 1400 pilots who stood alone against the might of Hitler's Germany during the dark summer of 1940—and gave England, in the words of Winston Churchill, "It's finest hour." Gone from the tarmac of British soil are the 17s, 24s, 47s, and 51s that terrorized the finest fighter squadrons the Luftwaffe had. Dimly remembered are the daring aviators that gave Americans some of their few proud moments in the skies over Korea. How fresh in the recall are the air commandos who valiantly struck the VC with their aging "Skyraiders" in the rain and blood soaked valley called A-Shau? And how long will be remembered the "Phantoms" and "Thuds" and "Buffs" over "Route Pack Six" and the flack filled skies of Hanoi? Barrel Roll, Steel Tiger, and Tally Ho. So here's a "Nickel on the Grass" to you, my friend, and your spirit, enthusiasm, sacrifice, and courage—but most of all to your friendship. Yours is a dying breed and when you are gone—the world will be a lesser place!

Friar Tuck
As printed in the *37th BS B-1b Squadron Songbook*

INTRODUCTION

It's been more than forty-three years since I deployed to Vietnam as a first lieutenant and pilot with the 389th tactical fighter squadron. I've told stories about my experiences (they get better with whiskey and age). My wife, Carole, began pestering me to write them down for my grandchildren. When the kids got old enough to read, I decided to recount my stories before they're lost forever.

I wrote about two hundred pages, surprised my memory hadn't faded too much. Then I mourned that I could only get my hands on three photographs from Vietnam, so Carole and I searched our basement. Together with some precious slides, we found over two hundred pages of letters I'd written to her during my tour. Despite my best housekeeping efforts, my incredible wife had protected them for almost half a century.

My old, brown, wrinkled letters! I couldn't have recaptured my thoughts without them. They reveal the emotions of a twenty-five-year-old romantic caught up in combat, separated from his young wife and son, badly missing his family, and trying to deal with the anxieties generated by warfare and an uncertain future. I want to share these private letters because they bring the story, the time, and the participants to vivid life.

I hadn't recorded every event chronologically in my first attempt at a memoir. The letters verified some dates, which were hard to remember. Some were wrong because Vietnam and the States are on opposite sides of the International Date Line; others because sometimes I wasn't sure what date, or even day of the week, it was.

I hadn't recorded every event accurately, either. Discrepancies existed between some events and my descriptions of them. Some of the inaccuracies were intentional. Soldiers must choose what to tell loved ones. As my tour progressed and missions got tougher, I purposely didn't share as much detail. Daily news accounts of lost planes and pilots were stressful enough for my family. But my attitude played a part, too. My initial thoughts of heroism were displaced by the grind of combat and futility of the war effort.

In the '60s an F-4 squadron consisted of about forty pilots. Their personalities ranged from wild and crazy to quiet and contemplative. The level of experience covered a wide range, too—from aircraft commanders with combat tours in two wars (World War II and the Korean War) to first lieutenants right out of pilot training, like me, who served as copilots (guys in back, or GIBs). We were a group of ordinary Americans who had chosen the exciting job of flying fighters. Our common denominators were the desire to fly fighters and the training process we had to pass to do so. Each of us was determined to do the job . . . some at all costs.

How calloused we became! How comfortable with a highly dangerous job! I often worried more about my family than myself. As I look back, once more I'm in the cockpit with a mighty F-4 "strapped on." With the bullets coming at us, these were our priorities:

First, **stay alive.** Do everything you can to survive.

Second, **protect your wingman.** He deserves your support; you need his.

Last (way after the first two), **accomplish the mission.**

Anything else is BS.

The comrades I served with were, for the most part, good men. One became my lifelong friend. One became a prisoner of war for more than six years. Another lost a leg. Two didn't come home. Why them? I had only a few close calls.

I now understand, after forty-some years, the price we paid serving our country. Killing and conflict scribe permanent marks on the subconscious, dark places to be revisited at some peril. Reading these long-forgotten letters reawakened the love I had for my family, but also the bile of death and destruction. Many of my comrades keep these memories from those who were never combatants. To this day I still tear up when I view fallen warriors. I can't control it and often try to hide it. I don't know why. Maybe my subconscious knows.

We took an oath to protect and defend our country. We followed orders, destroyed our targets, and flew the missions in spite of faulty tactics and, at times, poor leadership. Our job was not to question policies or politics, which wasted some good men's lives. Like most ordinary people caught in the vise of combat, we didn't have a lust for killing. We knew what tactics would allow us to defeat our foes. We fought hard, knowing that the more we hurt the enemy, the sooner we could all go home. We thought we were knights of the battlefield, but found out we were merely pawns of war.

We were motivated primarily by close comradeship, a bond few experience. That motivation kept us climbing into our cockpits day after day, often to face what were then the heaviest air defenses in the world. A lot of hardworking troops supported our planes and made it possible for us to do our jobs, but we still became elitists. We didn't suffer fools who were noncombatants and negatively affected our missions and lives. We called them "staff pukes."

These experiences forged my adult character. I became a realist and a believer in fate. I developed a lifelong disdain for liars, bureaucrats, glory seekers, and leaders who think only of themselves, and authoritarian types who think they're right just because they're boss. I hate arbitrary rules of any kind.

The harsh realities of armed conflict impose personal, internal conflict. Politicians, inept leaders, and noncombatants continue to create conflict for those of us at the tip of the mighty spear that is our military. Our families pay a price as well. They receive no medals for their courage, despite the heavy cost of long separations on young families. My wife—all our wives—displayed a special strength, dealing alone with family, finances, and homes, and living in fear of what each day's news might bring. I learned during my R and R trip to Hawaii how heavy a burden eight months of war had been on Carole. Some marriages failed. Thankfully, mine did not.

Events for a fighter pilot are swift. One second you might be safe, the next facing your destiny. Fighter jocks willingly operate daily within the thin margins of control and safety. Often someone else's instantaneous decision, a split second, or a few feet are the difference between life and death.

Rarely do I still dream about combat. But those fleeting seconds are burned deep into my physical memory. I can feel the adrenaline again. Gut reactions that flowed so rapidly at the time, but lasted only moments. The jumbled and broken bits are difficult to fashion into cohesive thought, which makes writing about them difficult. Four decades later it's still easier to portray life on the ground . . . to remember the humor and highjinks we used as a psychic tonic for the stresses of war.

Much has certainly been lost or faded with the passage of time. As my words unfold, my memory, though faulty, spins with more than I can write. Please forgive me. Forty years is a long time. I apologize also to my comrades in arms for any errors or omissions. I've edited names with discretion. And I thank those who contributed to my recollections and to this book.

This is what I now recall, and these are some of the letters I wrote home.

Gary Thrasher 2009

BOOK ONE:
THE 389TH DEPLOYS

1. The Adventure Begins—March 12, 1966

The sun rose over Alamogordo, New Mexico. Dawn crept cautiously along the shoulders of the Sierra Blanca Peak, a thin halo of light outlining its rim. Darkness lingered on the desert below.

I was in the rear seat of an F-4 Phantom. My aircraft commander, Captain Jimmy G. Martin, sat in front of me. Sweat trickled down our backs. We were dressed in rubber exposure suits. Uncomfortable. But we were anxious to begin our flight.

We were going to war.

I grew up in Bellevue, Nebraska, and attended the University of Nebraska in Lincoln. I worked my way through school with an assortment of jobs—factory worker, cutlery salesman, busboy, grocery clerk. I was always looking for more income.

The U.S. Air Force had a scholarship program as part of its Reserve Officers' Training Corps program. All you had to do was sign up for ROTC in your junior year, graduate, and serve four years as an officer, or five if you went into pilot training. Pilots got an extra hundred dollars per month flight pay, plus the Air Force paid for private pilot lessons during senior year. Cool! At the age of twenty-two, five years seemed like nothing.

In 1962, my junior year, I signed up. My true love, Carole, whom I'd dated in high school, was attending the University of Colorado. I'd just given her my fraternity pin (after she dumped a guy named Joe).

February 11, 1962

Dear Carole,

This is old stationery, not new; I have been writing you with it since I was a pledge. My brothers and Dad have brown eyes, my sister and mother green-blue, and I hope you know what color mine are. The rumor in ROTC has it that the OEP [Office of Education Planning] may be passed by Congress, and I could receive $1,100 next year.

Guess what the [monthly] pay scale is for 2nd Lts. with under two years longevity?

BASE PAY	$222.30
(This is only part subject to income tax.)	
FLIGHT PAY	100.00
SUBSISTENCE	47.88
QUARTERS ALLOWANCE	85.00
(If you do not live on base housing.)	
TOTAL	**$455.18**

This means my take-home pay would be a little over $400. Seems like a fortune compared to my income now. Most officers say they had more money as 2nd Lts. than they do now as Majors, etc. (or it seemed that way)!

You seem to be committing yourself when you want to know my family's eye chart. Recent reaction from the "brothers": "She isn't going to be here for the 'Pigge'" "Are you going?" "Is she Catholic?" "Lutheran?" "Six hundred miles is a long way." "Long time until Easter vacation." That is what it sounds like around here. For my part, when we have nice, warm sunny days like today, spring fever sure is a problem. Oh! Other quotes: "You must love her." "She must love you." And I have figured out our "fatal" attraction to each other: You girl—me boy (profound). Also, opposites attract. We do have several things in common (which is necessary); we also have differences, but these differences counter each other and develop a fuller person out of the two of us. It's almost like two elements forming a different compound, but in this case each retains its identity—which is affected by the association with the other—and I think it's wonderful!

I'm glad you were fair with Joe—it's better for him, and I think that you are sincere even though you refer to yourself as a "bastard"! Every man wants to see something of "elfishness" in a girl—you are the right combination of intelligent calamities that would make life very interesting. (Does it seem to you that I have been affected by philosophy or is it just my imagination?) By writing you, I may turn out to be one of the most prolific existential writers of our time—like modern Thomas Jefferson or Ben Franklin (pragmatic dreamer). The only thing that bothers me is that I realize writing you can't make Easter come any faster. E=mc^2 might help me out!

This letter may arrive on Valentine's Day—and it may be your only valentine if I forget to buy one tomorrow. However, my picture should be arriving any time, and that's the best valentine I could give. Sure wish I had one like that. Tomorrow for sure I must go to the central reserve area of the library (Love) and read two of my outside assignments. I have been dreading going over there and searching and asking where the area is, then where the books are, etc. You see, I have not checked a book out of our library and don't even know what's going on, except in the social sciences periodicals section and Moody's Industrial listings. Bad, isn't it? But just something I never get around to doing. Can I help it if the library just doesn't swing? Too many camel jockeys over there for me.

Well, running out of room and have a sudden inspiration to write "Ode to a red head," so will see if I can come up with anything and will mail with this letter.

Love, Gary

A high school and fraternity buddy, Pat Manrose, moved our romance along when he told Carole all the girls in Angel Flight were after me because I was commander of the cadet ROTC wing. A big man on campus. During our senior year Carole transferred to Nebraska and we got more serious. I didn't stand a chance!

I graduated from college, married Carole, and got commissioned in the U.S. Air Force all in the same month—May 1963. I bought a Corvette Stingray, a fighter pilot's car, for fifty dollars over dealer's cost from a fraternity brother's grandfather's dealership. The Bank of Bellevue loaned the newly minted lieutenant 100 percent of the purchase price and agreed not to require payments until I started active duty in September.

Carole and I spent the summer working at her parents' bar and living in the apartment above. She waitressed and I tended bar. Our special treat was to make chicken in the bar fryers, combine Black Label beer and tomato juice, and watch Combat! on TV. I had little idea how these events would shape the rest of my life.

I was assigned to a pilot training class at Laughlin AFB, Del Rio, Texas, and finished fourth in my class of over thirty student pilots. We listed our preferences, in rank order, for aircraft assignments after training. The higher a student's class standing, the better chance he had to receive his choice. I chose fighters. My first choice was the F-4.

My hometown of Bellevue was next to Offutt AFB. I used to ride my bike to a small junkyard on the base perimeter. One day I found a P-51 fuselage—no engine, no wings, but it had a stick and a five-gallon bucket for a seat. I flew a lot of make-believe missions in that Mustang, shooting down a lot of enemies. Now I wanted the real thing.

The Air Force was just about to make operational a hot new Navy fighter, the F-4 Phantom. They flew one to Laughlin AFB to give the student pilots a look. It was love at first sight, just as it was at the end of the eighth grade when I first saw Carole, the girl with the green eyes. My wife of over forty-six years.

The F-4 is big and ugly. It has a bulbous nose, bent-up wings, and a droopy tail. No clean lines. But it's a powerful bird with big engines. They're so powerful you could mount them on a Caterpillar D6 bulldozer, tilt the blade up, and fly. In its time the F-4 set world altitude and speed records. Its only drawback: it had two seats. I had to start off in the rear as a guy in back. A GIB! But what the hell? I had time. There wasn't a war on.

On the ramp at Holloman AFB in New Mexico, all extraneous thoughts fled my brain as the quiet of dawn was shattered by an auxiliary power unit coughing to life, blue flames bursting from its exhaust. As the APU powered up our aircraft, cockpit gauges sprang to life. We were ready to start engines.

Our squadron, the 389th Tactical Fighter Squadron (TFS), had just returned from a three-month deployment to Alaska when eighteen of our F-4 fighters were deployed to Vietnam. Our three sister squadrons of the 366th Tactical Fighter Wing (TFW)—the 390th, 391st, and 480th—were already deployed to Cam Ranh Bay and Danang in South Vietnam. We were going somewhere else but didn't know where.

Our mission was to fly to Hawaii, meeting KC-135 tankers en route. Aerial refueling would be necessary several times in flight. We wore exposure suits because we'd fly over at least an hour's worth of Pacific Ocean cold enough for regulations to mandate their use. We weren't happy about it. We'd be strapped in our fighters for about twelve hours and the suits would make us even more uncomfortable. We'd rather have taken our chances over the Pacific without them. Fighter pilots like to measure their own risks, not rely on the judgment of others.

For our trip we each had a box lunch and a thermos of coffee.

After we emptied the thermos it'd be our relief bottle. There was no other place to put urine except inside the exposure suits. I wondered how the coffee would taste on the next leg of the trip.

As we taxied to the end of the runway, eager for life's biggest adventure, our wives, families, and friends gathered to give us a final send off. They carried "Good Luck" signs and balloons, blew farewell kisses, and waved. Hearts heavy, we waved back.

As we taxied, I searched the crowd for Carole and my son, Brad, not yet two. I couldn't spot her. Damn! She was habitually late, but how could she miss this? Then I saw her—standing alone, several yards from the others. Brad was in a rucksack on her back. She held a sign, "Beware chicken pox," explaining her self-imposed quarantine.

Was this the last image I'd have of my family? I hoped not.

2. Felix Fowler

My war and that of my comrades in the 389th was made bearable by our squadron commander, then a major, Felix Fowler. Felix was a big man, about six feet four and 230 pounds. He was also a big man in many other ways. He wasn't preoccupied with his next promotion—he'd been a major for fourteen years. He had a genuine concern for his troops. He was a fine leader. And he was unflappable.

Felix had flown B-24 bombers in World War II. After the war he was a Cleveland cop for a few years. He enjoyed telling us he was the smallest guy on the "goon squad." He knew all the burglar's tricks of the trade. When the Korean War started, he was recalled to the Air Force and flew F-80s. Vietnam was his third war. No one could bullshit this man about air battle.

When I first arrived at Holloman AFB in New Mexico, Felix was the number two man in my squadron. Ray Obenshain, a lieutenant colonel, commanded the 389th.

One night, over the White Sands Missile Range, I was in Obenshain's backseat. We were running night beam radar intercepts with another F-4, taking turns as the bogey—the target. As we flew a series of diamond-shaped patterns, strange lights appeared above our ships each time we converged.

Obenshain instructed me to find the bogey above us on radar. I searched up 60 degrees but got no return on anything. Finally he called our ground radar controller.

"Do you have any other traffic out here with us?"

"You are the only two aircraft cleared in this airspace," the controller replied. "I see no other traffic."

The colonel lit the afterburners and climbed. We were light on fuel. The weird lights still hovered over us. I couldn't find them on radar and could only see them through the top of my curved Plexiglas canopy. The altimeter showed us above fifty thousand feet, the highest altitude I ever reached in an F-4. I was a little concerned about losing a canopy—we had no pressure suits on, so it would be curtains for both of us. Finally, standing on our tail, we fell out of the sky, completely out of air speed. Obenshain recovered nose down and got us flying again.

The entire time we were zooming after the bogey, the ground controller was on the radio asking what we were doing. Obenshain wouldn't tell him. Out of fuel, we headed back to base as Obenshain gave me my orders.

"Keep your mouth shut, lieutenant, or I will kick your ass!"

I did. I didn't tell anyone till several years after I'd left the Air Force.

Was it a UFO? One of our own top-secret birds playing with a couple of F-4s in the dark? All I know for sure is that I saw lights above me distorted by my canopy, and those lights could outclimb an F-4.

Two days later Colonel Obenshain had a massive heart attack and Felix got command of our squadron.

3. Alaska

Our squadron was the first in the 366th TFW to get F-4s. We passed an operational readiness test and deployed to Alaska in September 1965. For three months Felix led us. Not hamstrung by rules and regulations, he did what he thought best for his squadron of 350 men. He also taught us to accept challenges.

Home base was Alaskan Air Command headquarters, Elmendorf AFB in Anchorage. We were guests, on temporary duty to replace their F-102s sitting on five-minute alert. The Air Force sent its finest, fastest interceptor to meet the Russian reconnaissance bombers that often penetrated this remote airspace. We were there to photograph them. The rules of engagement were that we could not shoot unless shot at—and had to bring the bullet holes home to prove it.

Alaskan Air Command kept a suit of armor on a heavy stand as their totem. It was decorated with their unit insignia and brought out for formal occasions at the officers' club. They named it Iron Mike and jealously protected it from marauding visitors.

Felix bet the local F-102 squadron commander two cases of scotch that the 389th could steal Iron Mike. All he needed were some accomplices. He chose our flight surgeon, who had the use of a four-wheel-drive ambulance outfitted with stretchers that could be used to carry it. He also chose four young lieutenants to carry the stretcher: Larry Day, Fred Frostic, Bob Winegar, and me. He asked two of us to scout out the club and jimmy the doors. He showed us his burglar tricks from Cleveland.

We went to the club. Under Felix's direction, Fred and I taped a thin wire behind a side-door lock, leaving just enough wire protruding to grab with a pair of pliers and pull from behind the lock. Thus, we could open the "locked" door in about ten seconds. We returned to barracks and set our alarms for four in the morning.

When we met up with our flight surgeon, designated driver of the getaway ambulance, he was nervous despite Felix's assurances. Ambulance lights off, we pulled up to the rear of the club. From the parking lot we could see into the room with Iron Mike.

A night watchman sat at a desk reading, Iron Mike directly across from him. We four lieutenants were crestfallen. Our mission was foiled.

"What can we do?" we asked Felix.

"We'll have to mug him," Felix responded. "Get some tape and a sheet and we'll throw it over his head."

The flight surgeon just about shit. He bailed out of the ambulance and we never saw him again that night. Bob Winegar took his place as driver. Felix and his remaining accomplices got out of the ambulance, adhesive tape, sheets, and stretcher in hand.

As we four silently crept through the darkness, we saw the watchman rise from his chair, stretch, and head into the bathroom. Now was our chance! We pulled the door jimmy through the lock, burst down the hall, and put Iron Mike on the stretcher. Excitedly, we raced to the ambulance, opened the rear doors, and thrust him in.

"Let's go! Let's go!" we lieutenants exclaimed.

Felix was calm. "No. I want to see this."

We huddled in the ambulance, waiting for the watchman. His business done, he returned to his desk, sat down, and picked up his book—then did the biggest double take I've ever seen. He jumped up and looked all around the room. He'd been away only a few minutes, but Iron Mike was gone. Lucky for him he'd only been burgled, not mugged. We drove off howling.

We hid our prize in a missile case in our hangar. The next day Felix sent orders to the F-102 commander and the Alaskan Command, transferring Iron Mike to our squadron. For the rest of our tour we hid Iron Mike from the air police. Felix assigned a lieutenant every day to guard him from the extensive effort launched to recover him. To rub it in, we took him out at night from time to time and shot Polaroid pictures of him at every recognizable place on base. We sent them to our foes.

Iron Mike was recaptured by the Alaskan Command when fifty air police made a sweep of our squadron hangar. A reporter from the Seattle Post–Intelligencer got wind of the story. Iron Mike was stolen several times subsequently and ended up being flown around the world. He now resides in the U.S. Air Force Museum at Wright-Patterson AFB. He wears a 389th TFS patch!

Felix decided that the young pilots in the backseat deserved some flights as aircraft commander, AC, with an instructor pilot in the rear seat. The Iron Mike capture team members were the first new lieutenants assigned to the squadron after F-4 school. We four were picked to start our upgrade to AC. We didn't know then that we'd make our final transition to F-4 AC under combat conditions.

Larry, Fred, and Bob were Air Force Academy graduates. They were smart, motivated, top-notch guys who went on to have accomplished careers. Larry became a major general, Fred an assistant secretary of defense, and Bob a respected radiologist. They're among the finest men I have known and I'm proud to have had such comrades and friends.

I will never forget the thrill of my first ride up front in an F-4. I flew a clean bird—no external fuel tanks—and in the cold Alaskan air it performed like a rocket ship. For a twenty-five-year-old, nothing can beat free gas and the ability to roam at will over some of the most scenic land on earth in the world's best fighter.

Felix gave the local F-102 squadron a chance to win back their scotch. Two weeks before our return to New Mexico he wrote down the tail numbers, take-off times, and crew names in the exact order we would launch to return home. For him to win the bet there could be no variance—which meant no problems with any of the eighteen birds or their crews.

Everyone in the squadron knew about the bet. Our crew chiefs and maintenance guys worked like beavers to keep our craft airworthy. We aircrews worked to stay healthy. It would be a tremendous accomplishment.

Before dawn, in the pitch black of Alaska in December, we taxied eighteen F-4s in the planned sequence to the end of the runway—in a blinding snowstorm with minimal visibility. One by one, on time and in order, we followed Felix's lead plane and launched into the night. Felix had given us the great pride and desire to perform as a unit.

After a long flight back to Alamogordo, New Mexico, Felix throttled back and orbited his flight of four. Low on fuel, he circled, throttles at minimum, while the rest of the squadron, which had been strung out during the return journey, raced to join formation before we all ran out of fuel. We made a full-squadron, eighteen-ship, tight diamond formation fly-by, low over the base. The 389th had returned. Everyone on base and in Alamogordo would know.

We were as close personally as we were in tight formation. We were a motivated team. We would follow Felix anywhere.

Our wing had received orders to deploy to Vietnam. The war was escalating. The Air Force was sending its top fighter into the fray. Our squadron was ready.

4. Guam, Russians, and Delays

On day one of our deployment to Vietnam, we flew from Alamogordo to Hawaii. On day two, Hawaii to Guam. This boy from the flatlands of Nebraska soon found out that the Pacific is a huge ocean. I spotted several Navy ships far below and was glad to be cruising at over five hundred knots, not their sixteen. It had been two long days flying behind tankers with nothing to do but follow loose formation and daydream, except when actually refueling behind a tanker.

Our first morning on Guam we still didn't know our ultimate destination. We found out during our final briefing that our new base would be Phan Rang. We'd never heard of it and rushed to the maps. The base was still under construction. The runway would be completed just hours before our arrival.

One of our planes broke an aileron actuator and parts had to be flown in from the States. One crew on test flight status needed to stay behind to test fly the bird after repairs. Martin and me. I was disappointed. I wanted to arrive with the squadron.

We waited a day or two until the plane was repaired. Then we went up for a test hop. Everything checked out on the repair job, so we had extra fuel and nothing to do but play. The Russians had a spy trawler off Guam to monitor our activity. So we went looking for Russians.

We found their ship and decided to give them some simulated gun passes. We flew over low, very low. They waved; we gave them the finger. I wished we had a gun and ammo. They were helping the enemy in Vietnam.

The unexpected delay put me in a financial bind. I was short on cash and never heard of a credit card. I wrote to Carole.

16 March 66
From Guam

> Hello from the South Pacific. I still am not in Viet Nam, but instead on the rock pile called Guam. Jimmy and I had a fuel counter problem in Hawaii so we were there two days and the rest of the squadron went on. We only had a few hours to see the island and the beach because no one was sure when our bird would be fixed. So we went on to Guam and found that one of the other planes ahead of us was broke and needing a part and test hop, so Wilson and Caverly took ours and we have been here almost three days now while the rest of the squadron is in Phan Rang.
>
> There is not much to do on this island, and I'm beginning to run short of coins. I was not planning on taking so long to arrive in Vietnam. If the part doesn't get here for a couple of days or we don't have a tanker right away, I may have

to cash a check on the Bellevue Bank for $50 or so. If I do, I'll send you a telegram so you can make the necessary arrangements to cover the check in the bank.

We just got back from the beach sunburned, but it was really beautiful. There is not much to do on this small island, but drinks are only 25 and 30 cents for V.O. at the club and the food is good and inexpensive, not to mention the good service given by the native waiters. This is where all the B-52s make their bombing runs on Vietnam. Wish I could fight the war from here too—it would be great. But I guess we will have to finish the trip all the way. I hope I get reimbursed for all the money it is costing me to eat . . . and the BOQ [bachelor officers' quarters] fees along with everything else, like having to buy a $50 pair of shoes in Hawaii because I left mine in the middle of the living room . . . So don't be surprised if you get a telegram from me and maybe I'll send one whenever I get a chance.

How is Brad? Does he miss me, or can you tell? I miss you both and love you too. Keep me in your thoughts and keep care of yourselves.

It is funny seeing all of these islands, Pearl Harbor, and places in the Pacific where men were fighting a war twenty-five years ago. It seems sad that we are on our way to do it all again—the ocean is so big and beautiful and the islands so much like paradise it seems foolish to use them and travel over them for war. Too bad we are not perfect. How have all the wives taken it? I am not sure I spotted you and Brad as we were taxiing out to leave. There was a big group of people there.

Keep your chin up and take good care of my boy. I know you can do many good things while I am gone if you only work at it a little and don't let people feel sorry for you.

The next day we got our own tanker for the flight to Phan Rang. En route we took turns refueling. Gassing up from an airborne tanker wasn't tough if you had smooth air. It was just close air formation flying, something fighter pilots did a lot of nearly every day.

Martin was good about letting me fly. He was an excellent pilot and I knew I'd learn a lot from him. He was also a fine man, easygoing and unflappable in combat.

We were motivated to do a good job refueling. If we didn't offload from the tanker we'd probably have to ditch in the ocean, even though the flight plan said we might make it to some small island out there somewhere. That part of the flight plan didn't have our confidence, but all went as planned.

After about ten hours we saw the coast of South Vietnam off our nose. Many thoughts flowed through my mind. *What will our base be like? What will our primary missions be? Will the enemy defenses be tough? Can I handle being shot at? Will I be afraid? Will I live through my tour in Vietnam?*

My tour was supposed to last a year.

BOOK TWO:
PHAN RANG

389TH BASES IN SOUTH VIETNAM
LAOS
CAMBODIA
DA NANG
PHANG RANG
SAIGON

5. Welcome to the War

Martin and I were finally over Phan Rang, just southwest of Cam Ranh Bay, next to a small coastal fishing village. Our base had been a World War II Japanese airfield. Below us our engineers had scraped the earth raw, a red scar on the verdant landscape. Two nearby hills were leveled, the rock used for the foundation of a new ten-thousand-foot runway. A pipeline running here from the shore would provide the thousands of gallons of fuel our birds would need. In a few months the Americans altered the landscape more than the Vietnamese had in hundreds of years. I wondered how much more we would change their country.

The runway was built of interlocking aluminum plates. Unlike the pierced steel planking used throughout the Pacific in World War II, the plates had no holes but had a rubber and grit coating for traction, which nevertheless proved slick after a rain. Rainwater could seep through the plates, eventually eroding the supporting earth below. Our sixty-thousand-pound loads rolling over the aluminum created potholes that threatened to swallow our aircraft.

The taxiways and runway needed frequent repairs.

Martin and I landed. We opened the canopies and were engulfed in heat, dust, and humidity. Martin parked on a large open ramp and shut down the engines. The place was alive with activity. Construction was going on all around us. The bulk of our squadron had already started flying combat missions.

"Welcome to Vietnam," our crew chief greeted us.

Days before, when our squadron arrived, they were given a big reception. Generals, local officials, Vietnamese girls with leis, a band, and photographers all turned out to greet them. Only a bare-chested crew chief noticed our arrival, and he was more interested in his plane.

A single, helmeted air police guard, with radio and M-16 rifle, stood his solitary watch inside a sandbagged foxhole on the corner of the ramp. A simple, flimsy plywood roof shielded him from the broiling sun. He had to endure the heat as well as the noise and dust blown up by aircraft and construction machinery. He, too, had a tough job.

The ramp was like a griddle, the sun heating it to well over 100 degrees. I felt it through the soles of my combat boots as I walked. The heat, retained at night, attracted poisonous snakes, which crawled out to savor the latent warmth, hiding near our wheels and chocks. I soon discovered that pre-flighting my aircraft on dark mornings could be an adventure. Once I bent down under a wing, my flashlight illuminating the wheel. Beside it, head flared, a king cobra warned me I was disturbing his rest. Setting the world's backward broad jump record, I hit my head on the underside of the wing and landed flat on my back beyond the aircraft tail. In a few weeks the snakes tired of our noisy intrusion and retreated to quieter snake places.

Helmets and map cases in hand, Martin and I walked to our squadron operations tent adjacent to the ramp. Eight pilots composed the crew complement of a flight of four. We operated from tents with dirt floors, rolling up the sides to let the stifling heat escape and quickly lowering them when the afternoon thunderstorms hit. Often it took all eight pilots hanging on tent poles to keep them from blowing away during mission briefings.

Inside the operations tents were large, plywood credenzas about eight feet long, flown in from New Mexico, that had many panels, mounting maps, weapon setting charts, and so on. These were great inside buildings in New Mexico, but Vietnam's rain and humidity soon warped and split them, making them unusable. We tossed them outside to make more room for air to circulate. We trashed a lot of things there.

Martin and I found our personal equipment tent and stowed our flight gear on the metal racks from the States. We were immediately put on the schedule to fly the next day and then sent to our housing area, a tent city about three miles from the flight line.

We rode in the back of a compact Ford Econoline pickup. Each flight had one for transportation. We soon passed four newly arrived Army privates hoofing along the road, duffle bags over their shoulders. Their assignment was the 101st Airborne, whose base of operations was just southwest of our airfield. We offered the eighteen-year-olds a ride. They threw their gear in the bed and hopped in after it.

"What do you fly?" they asked Martin and me.

"Phantoms."

"How fast do they go?"

"One thousand, six hundred fifty miles an hour," I said, giving them my personal best groundspeed from Alaska. That always impressed an eighteen-year-old. To me, a mature twenty-five, they looked like kids. Fresh from basic infantry training, after a couple of weeks conditioning in the heat of the jungle they'd be on the battlefield. Some would return old men.

We dropped them off near their base and received a "Thanks, and good luck!" and a salute.

6. Life in a Hootch

Hot and dusty, we arrived at our housing area, where we were to live in hootches—glorified tents, with wooden floors and plywood halfway up the side walls, topped by screens. Rain blew into them almost every afternoon.

A hootch housed six men, each assigned a personal cubbyhole equipped with a metal locker and a wooden footlocker to stow belongings, a couple of bare electric bulbs, and an outlet. Our hootch had only five pilots.

We found our gear on two cots. Our B-4 bags, containing our clothes, had been flown in by transports, along with the tons of material needed to equip our squadron. The bags were already saturated with red dust. The earth here was bright red, much like Oklahoma. The thunderstorms made red mud. In no time all of our belongings turned some shade of red, even our underwear.

24 March 66
Hootch 1005, Phan Rang

Dear Hon and Son,

Well, finally made it to S.V.N. Phan Rang looks like some John Wayne WW II movie set. It is unbelievable the amount of equipment, material, and men assembled here. Believe it or not this area is almost like Alamogordo, only worse because the humidity is high due to the nearness of the ocean. It is so unbelievably hot and humid (Ninety-eight degrees when we landed this afternoon) that you just roll in sweat even standing still. Our part came into Guam Monday, and we finally got a tanker today. Good thing, too, because I have to borrow money to live on the rest of the month, and I hope I get paid at the end of the month. I am sorry I had to wire you for some money but it was the least amount possible I could get by on. I am also sorry to hear that you are having to cash checks to buy groceries with. I had hoped that loan would keep all of us from hardship this month. I hope you found a way to get some money in the bank without too much trouble. I am also sorry I did not write more from Guam, but I had no stationery or stamps and did not want to borrow all of Jimmy's. Anyway, there was not much to write about—nothing on Guam, especially with little money and only one shirt and pair of pants. So please forgive me and keep on writing. Don't get mad and stay—the main reason I was anxious to get here was I knew I would have mail waiting for me from you.

Here it is hard to believe I am actually in a war—almost. Right now there's artillery firing in the distance and two days ago a Vietnamese outpost was overrun five miles from here.

Everyone who has flown here likes it because they are getting to see some results of all the practice we have been doing.

Things are really crude and basic—open latrines—showers—and we are living in half-frame, half-tent structures we call "hootches." They have a canvas roof with plywood screen sides and screen doors installed by us.

Jimmy and I are living with Kovar, Womack, and Murphy—we have cots with lumpy mattresses and sheets, and we spent the day today building steel two-door wardrobes, which are really nice for clothes. We also have another footlocker so things are not too bad for storage. Mildew should not be too much of a problem with the heat either. I am thirsty all the time, and one of the greatest preoccupations around here is getting cold drinks. There are plenty of soft drinks, etc. but ice is a big problem. I just returned from the shower and a fan makes things better. My fan is running but the plastic case cracked in shipment. But it runs good.

Local Vietnamese women work on base during the day and clean our hootches—sweeping the floor mainly. They also do our laundry every day, so at least we won't be completely filthy (although I must say everyone looks pretty rough around the edges right now).

Everyone seems in good spirits here and morale is very good, so things are going to be OK here.

I'm sorry if things are rough for you right now financially, but get a loan if things are too tough, and I will try to send you some money as soon as I can get paid. This will never happen again, I promise. I am proud of you and my son—glad you are not a recluse and are out doing things already. I like to know that you can do so well while I am away. It is never good to be away and I am glad I only have to worry as to whether you will have enough money.

I really deeply love you and never seem to feel it as much as when I am away. Take good care of my son, and I hope he keeps growing big and will still remember me when I come home.

Love, Gary

Over the next few weeks my hootchmates and I scrounged up lumber to add some amenities. We built shelves, a washstand at the rear, and a bar. We redefined comfortable living. We had no running water—to shave or wash you got a pan of water from one of the two-wheeled tankers on our dusty street. We often shaved in early morning darkness by the single bulb over our washstand. The light attracted numerous swarming bugs. Before you finished, your shaving cream was peppered with them.

Between the hootches were bomb shelters—just a circle of sandbags about shoulder height with an open top. There was no top protection against mortars, but we weren't alarmed. We hadn't seen a mortar attack. Our protection was our side arms, kept close at hand, and a machine gun nest manned by two air police on the hilltop just above our living quarters.

John Critzberg, who lived in the end hootch, one day decided to anchor our defenses. He cut an opening in the floor of his hootch and dug a hole—his hidey hole—and equipped it with a case of grenades he got from our Army friends. Nobody dropped in to visit him, as he'd often toss an entering visitor a live grenade.

At night the 101st Airborne fired 105 mm howitzers over Nui Dot, the hill just behind us, to try to keep the Vietcong wary of coming closer. The shells normally arced over Nui Dot and hit a few miles away, scaring monkeys and keeping the Vietcong alert.

Nighttime was also letter-writing time.

25 March 66
Hootch 1005

Dear Hon and Son,

Well, I am now officially moved in. Your picture is up on a shelf I built. I guess I will have lots of time to organize, organize, and reorganize. We are getting the place modified and it is beginning to look nice. Today we put a ceiling up to try and keep the heat on the roof. . . . We have a cooler in the tent and ice is brought around every day if the ice machine is not broken or something. The dust is all over everything and we cover our beds with ponchos to catch it.

Our housemaid's name is My. She is a youngster and does not speak much English. I spent almost an hour today with her, trying to teach her English and learn some Vietnamese. God, what a mess. Anyway it is a necessity because we have to pantomime what we want her to do, but she does good work and it is convenient to have your laundry done every day. You could go through about six sets of clothes a day here—you start sweating at nine in the morning and do not stop until night.

Just finished a trip to our eight-holer and the shower and feel pretty good. Still do not know when I will be paid, but as soon as I get some money in my pocket to live on, I will make you another allotment for my flight pay, $125, then you will have something to save and a little more for fun.

We went to the town of Phan Rang today, population 25,000, and it surprised me. The people are very energetic and everyone was busy. They have lots of schools and the children are really cute. The girls wear white silk gowns with some over-blouse or something in beautiful colors. Jimmy and I are equipped now. We bought commando hats to keep the sun off and a bamboo floor mat to keep beside the bed. He also bought a wash bowl and mirror so now we are all set to keep house.

By the way, in Vietnamese mother is "Ma" and a young unmarried son is "Em." I spent a few minutes pointing out your picture and learning the Vietnamese pronunciation—they have several inflections of the same word with different meanings. I am a "Chung Gui"—a first lieutenant. Captain Martin is "Dai Gui." All the Vietnamese use the expression "number one" for very good, and "number ten" bad, and number ten thousand worse, etc. We ran into a boy downtown who could speak English and he was quite a character—served as our guide and he had a ball trying to get us to speak Vietnamese.

The people are very friendly and gracious and interesting. So I hope I can learn a lot of their language and customs, if possible, while I am here. There are so many things to see and purchase that I wish you were here so I could buy you some black PJs. But the war is real—on certain roads we can not turn right at the intersection because the VC (Viet Cong) control it and they are all around the place and you cannot recognize them until they fire at you.

All my love to you and my Buddy Boy. I will try to write two pages every day.

P.S. I fly twice tomorrow.

Love, Gary

The next evening I wrote about my first combat mission. (I called Carole "Heatherton" because she had her hair cut short like that television personality.)

26 March 66

Dear "Heatherton" and Son,

Third day in a row on the letter writing, and I hope they don't arrive the same day. Flew our first combat missions today (2) and everything went well. All the practice pays off after all. From the air you can see fires and bomb craters everywhere so you wonder how we can't help but win eventually.

The red dust has turned to red mud tonight—we had a thunderstorm this afternoon before our second flight. I don't care for the mud but it cooled things off considerably, which was very welcome as the temperature was 100 degrees before the rain started. You can't believe how much we sweat going out to the airplane.

I take a G-suit, parachute harness, life preserver, pistol belt with pistol, canteen full of water, survival jacket with another pistol, flares, compass, first aid kit, radio, knife, strobe light, ammunition, etc., plus helmet, gloves, checklists, maps, etc. A person is literally surrounded with leather, canvas, metal, and perspiration. I must weigh at least 250 pounds, not counting the 65-pound survival kit I sit on in the bird.

So you can see we are really quite well prepared for any eventuality. We had steak tonight—Saturday night specials. They show movies down the street on the side of a "white elephant," which is an inflated rubber warehouse.

We just returned from our trip up the hill to the showers. It's the first time I have ever worn my combat boots to the shower, and it was quite a trip through the mud and darkness. The shower is really the high point of the day around here. It really feels good to get out of wet fatigues or smelly flight suit.

I am going to have to "forecast" pretty soon where I want to go in the States and overseas, plus what flying assignment I would like. I want to fly F-4s and will probably use Holloman and MacDill, in that order, as bases. For overseas—Germany and England for assignments. I don't know what to do about selling our house, even if I do return to the States.

7. A Night at the Movies

Our only entertainment was outdoor movies projected on the side of the "white elephant," a warehouse of white rubberized material kept inflated by air pressure from several fans. It was shaped like an oblong balloon—and of course tinged with red. Cinemascope movies projected on that convex surface made an interesting, distorted picture. We each had a folding metal chair in our hootch that we carried about a block to the movie. There was no popcorn.

One night I stayed home from the movie, reading on my cot, when I heard a big explosion, nearly overhead. An Army 105 mm shell fused over Nui Dot, exploding prematurely. I heard the metal chairs clanking and rapid footfalls as my comrades, thinking we were under attack, abandoned the movie for the bunkers next to the hootches. I wondered what my family was doing at that moment.

2 April 66

Dear Hon and Son,

Just finished watching the movie on the white elephant—*Irma La Douce* was on and wasn't as bad the second time. Flew again today, and twice on the schedule tomorrow, which is Sunday.

The chow has been dropping off in the mess hall this week, but I guess a big convoy came in from Cam Ranh Bay today. Lots of beer and sodas—too bad we haven't had any ice for three days now.

They are building a new shower just up the end of our street so we will have a shorter trip to relaxation every night. Right now it is 0530 Saturday morning in Alamogordo, and I often wonder what you and Brad are doing at the time I write each letter. I can picture both of you sleeping right now and wish I were home to put the covers on B and sleep with you. There is a fifteen-hour difference in time—I am fifteen hours ahead of you each day.

I really don't want you to get a job. It's bad enough B is without a father, so I feel he should have a full-time mother to make up for all the love I can't give him right now. Of course, I'll bet you get tired of him sometimes and I'll bet he really is dependent on you. You are his whole family right now.

It's cool again tonight and I should have a good sleep. I must be up at 0600, which is 5pm Alamogordo time. When you get this letter try and remember what you were doing at that time. I'll be thinking of you. Do you get my letters more than one at a time? If you do, I'll write every other day or so and then you will get one at a time.

Love, Gary

8. Care Packages

The bar in our hootch became our social center. Some American gave the local Vietnamese tinsmith the pattern for beer coolers and he made them of galvanized tin, exact replicas of those in the States. We purchased one from an American sergeant who became an entrepreneur. Each night, presuming ice was available, he filled up the back of a government pickup truck he borrowed for deliveries with blocks of ice procured off base. The blocks were hollow, because our demand for ice exceeded the local Vietnamese capacity to produce it, and were covered in a loose pile of empty rice hulls for insulation. Because the hulls coated the ice, it wasn't suitable for mixed drinks. If you wanted whiskey, you drank it neat. We also had a vague suspicion the ice might have been poisoned by an enthusiastic local guerrilla. As our vendor drove down our dusty tent row, water from melting ice poured from the back of the pickup. There was more money in ice used for U.S. beer than for fish at the local village. Capitalism at work! The only other ice on base was at the hospital.

The highlight of our day was delivery by the iceman. The sun baked our hootches, and every evening after chow we returned to them to strip down to skivvies and flip-flops. Waiting expectantly, we placed two beers apiece in the cooler. When the ice arrived we threw it on top of the beers and literally watched it melt before our eyes. The beer ended up cool, not cold, but was a small pleasure.

We stood around our bar trading comments about the events of the day and discussing the next day's missions. Guys from other hootches dropped by to swap tales. We shared care packages that arrived from our families. Our letters to them pleaded for snacks and goodies unavailable on base and they responded with vigor—cookies, cakes, crackers, candy, nuts, Vienna sausages, and, my personal favorite, potato chips.

We were like kids, eagerly opening newly arrived goodies from the States. Most things in soft boxes or packages came smashed and broken. One wife's cake, baked with love and care, arrived completely flattened, frosting melted. We devoured it anyway.

We swore that somewhere in the mail system a three-hundred-pound gorilla was assigned to jump on every package. My potato chips were always in fragments, but I persisted in asking for them. We learned over time that goodies packed in cans could survive the gorilla. Our suppliers back home got the message and become skilled at packing things in used tins.

Forty years later I used these tips when my youngest son, Trevor, served as a Green Beret in Iraq. Our family and friends sent him and the "Jundies" he trained much-valued personal items not available in the bush. I realized that there truly is much more pleasure in giving than receiving.

28 March 66, Hootch 1005

Dear Wife and Son,

Just finished chow and shower after flying my 6th combat mission in three days. It was cooler today, and the afternoon mission was almost bearable. The 101st Airborne, camped just southwest of us, kept me awake last night with their random artillery fire up into the hills. Also, Gary Baetz came by just as we were going to bed with the latest Cobra count and Scorpion tally. Jimmy heard snakes in our hootch all night. As a matter of fact, he just filled in two holes under our new front door because he was worried about creatures attacking us at night.

This morning we escorted some C-123s on a low-level mission in case someone fired at them, but we ended up dropping 500-pounders on a VC battalion in the woods. We sure made a lot of matchwood. Just being here already has gotten me two or three medals, and I only need twenty for an air medal. Col. Fowler also said that most people flying combat a year will probably get the DFC [Distinguished Flying Cross] also—so I'll look great when I get all of them on my blues. I am not anxious to get a purple heart added either. Going to walk down and see "Harlow." Finish tomorrow PM.

Same night, and everyone is restless after the movie. Just starting to rain now. I've got to be up at 0415 tomorrow. Early to bed, early to rise, etc. Mrs. Kovar sent a can of jalapeno bean dip and some tortilla chips—they hit the spot, so you can send us a care package anytime you can afford it. Hope B gets over his infant ailments soon so you can stop being the worried mother. I guess I'll fix you up with a little girl so you'll have your hands so full you won't have time to worry. I hope B doesn't get the mumps right after the pox. It's time for the little guy to have some fun and be healthy for a while. I am glad to hear I'll probably be TDY [temporary duty] for about 5 months in F-4 school. Maybe that is—who knows—I might even be upgraded here. I guess it won't be for a while, so write me and tell me where you would like to go if you still want to be married to a vagabond. Maybe the "wish list" will come true. Then maybe we can decide what to do with our cul-de-sac on Bellamah.

Have your plants died in your garden yet? I figure they are about done for now, if they follow your botanical schedule as usual. Brad sounds like quite the water boy.

Well, I'll only make about three pages tonight. I have to fly early tomorrow, and my filthy sheets are looking better as the day grows longer. As for mailing packages to me, here is my primary wish list right now: foil packages of lemonade and ice tea so we can make our own cool ones. You should get together with Louise and Mrs. Kovar and Womack on care package shipments so you don't all send the same thing. Some tall plastic drinking glasses wouldn't be bad.

P.S. Send me your zip code.

Love, Gary

My attitude about medals changed as the war progressed. I also thought I might come back to the States for upgrade training to aircraft commander in an F-4. Not only was there uncertainty about the war, there were also many unknowns about our future life, and where my next assignment might lead us.

9. Gourmet Mess Hall

We ate our meals on steel compartmentalized trays in a giant mess hall. The wash-up procedure consisted of standing in line and dipping the steel tray into a garbage can filled with hot soapy water, then a second with bleach and water. The garbage cans were heated by kerosene burners placed inside them, with a small chimney rising above. The heaters often lit with a blast of flame and a loud *whoomp*. You could easily spot the enlisted mess helpers. They were the guys with smudged faces and one or more eyebrows singed off.

For our first six weeks at Phan Rang we had a lot of powdered eggs, awful powdered coffee, and two main courses: canned mini hamburgers in a gray sauce and an unidentifiable meat that looked like corned beef.

Our highly trained military cooks did vary the menu. On day one they served mini hamburgers for breakfast, unidentifiable meat for lunch, and mini burgers at night. On day two, they served unidentifiable meat in the morning, mini burgers at noon, and unidentifiable meat at night. They repeated the menu for six weeks. We eventually got fresh meat and vegetables when refrigeration arrived.

10. Showers and Shitters

The common shower, located at the end of our row of hootches, was an enclosed wooden platform with a latticework of rough sawn planks laid over crushed rock. Moss soon grew on the planks. The plumbing was gravity-powered: water fell from a large, black tank that sat on top of the shower. The sun heated it. If you showered early, it was warm. Late arrivals got a cold shower.

The latrines were basically "piss pipes"—six-inch pipes set into the ground at about a 45 degree angle, just short of crotch height. Try hitting one of those in the dark! The smell of ammonia became strong enough to knock a maggot off a garbage truck.

The real treat was the eight-hole shitter, built of plywood and screened above the waist to keep the flies out. An entire flight could take a group shit, usually badly needed after taking one's weekly malaria pill, which frequently brought on cramps and diarrhea. More than one mission briefing ended with eight bare-assed pilots in the shitter.

Under each seat was a fifty-five-gallon drum cut in half to hold the waste. Trap doors on the side of the whole structure could be opened to remove the drums.

The worst job in Vietnam had to be the shit meister—the enlisted man who ran the crew of "mommy sans" that burned out the shitters. Mommy sans were skinny crones wearing conical straw hats, black pajamas, and flip-flops. They chewed betel nut and could spit like cowboys chewing tobacco. The betel nut juice turned their teeth black and their gums purple. Most were missing some teeth.

The shit meister drove a truck loaded with mommy sans, who used diesel fuel and gasoline to burn out the drums. It could get really uncomfortable when you were on the throne and a giggling mommy san opened up the trap door behind you and removed your drum. It got worse when she placed a hot one, just burned out, under your butt. Ouch! I suspected these beauties were closet Vietcong guerrillas.

11. Unit Pride

We had been in Vietnam less than two weeks but our squadron worked hard, flew a lot of missions, and had some good results, despite the lousy food and living conditions. Even as I remained idealistic and patriotic and expressed a lot of pride in my team, I was already seeing changes in myself and questioning war.

Carole had yet to receive a single one of my letters.

4 April 66

Dear Hon and Son,

Nine in the morning and the iceman finally came. I got two blocks just to make sure things would be cold for a couple of days. It would be great around here if we could get ice and letters every day. No maid has come on base for four days now. This week we haven't had any fresh food at the chow hall. Everything has been out of C-ration cans. Do you believe Spam sixteen different ways? I think they have even been reheating and reserving the stuff for two days—the result is that everyone here has the GIs this week. Yesterday Bob Atkinson and I had to get up in the middle of a briefing to shit. Everyone has the same problem, so there is no sympathy.

I managed to fly twice yesterday without incident. It reached 100 degrees again, but the nights are fairly cool now. My only problem with sleep has been the bugs—they seem to like me and I have to throw a dozen out of bed every night before I can get to sleep. They don't bite; they just like to crawl all over me.

We have a volleyball court up at the end of our street, so we can get some exercise in the evenings.

PM the 4th. Just returned from the shower, and once again I am a new man for a few hours. The iceman came today, and it sure is good to have a few cold beers in the hootch again. I guess a C-130 landed here this PM with 16,000 pounds of mail, so I should get a letter from you tomorrow. We have a pilots' meeting tonight at 7:30. I guess we will have them every Monday night while we are here.

We almost ran into a VNAF [Vietnam Air Force] forward air controller on our mission today. Jimmy got the windscreen fogged up on a napalm (jellied fuel fire bomb) pass, and couldn't see out front. I saw him and pulled up out of the road. Don't know what he was doing over our target anyway.

On the schedule twice tomorrow. I ate only once today, and the GIs seem to be subsiding now—not eating helps, I guess.

I'm reading *Catch 22* again—some good analogies to this place, and the military in it keeps me laughing. Has your mother moved into Alamogordo yet? I was sure she would be there by April. You can't have Brad all to yourself, you know—he is too precious for that.

Just returned from our pilots' meeting. Everyone was there. Word is that no one knows what any of the big plans are here, so we are all going to hang loose and try to make as many improvements as possible to better living conditions. Col. Talbott is very pleased with our performance so far. So am I. It almost seems amazing how we do our job here with the professional execution. I never would have believed that I'd so casually brief for a combat mission, or better yet, execute one with complete knowledge and confidence in every phase of the mission. All our training has paid off.

Don't worry about me too much. I only know of one mission that I've been shot at for sure, and usually there is none we know of. It's usually that way every mission, so we do a good job. The ground troops really like to see us soften up a patch of jungle or mangrove patch or landing zone for them. Several times over the radio, I've heard of air strikes completely suppressing enemy fire on our troops. Makes you feel good to know that you can really help.

This place really surprised me. We salute more over here than Stateside and everyone is closer—working harder. It's magnificent to see what men can do if they are called to do it. Everyone at home is fortunate to have such men to make sacrifices for them. I've never been prouder of my uniform and my peers than I am now.

We laugh and joke about the medals and ribbons we receive (six more missions and I'll have an air medal), but I know that, truly, inside myself and all the rest, we will be very proud to wear them because something has gone into each one. The effort each of us made puts not only some little ribbon on our chest, but also something more inside that chest, something I feel already. I know that it's tenuous and in the subconscious, but just the same I know that it will be there—and no one back home will have to recognize it, even if they could—for me to feel it.

I hope Brad will be able to feel it someday without going to a strange land and fighting strange people for a strange reason. War by itself . . . well, my small view of it right now seems strange. And when I fly over the land and look below, I wonder why MAN has to do this to one another. God, I bet this letter really sounds bad! My being philosophical is something to endure. But I feel that I'm communicating with you, and we never talk about this subject here. It's better to be detached and perform the mechanics of our job.

Ten p.m. and mail call. The mail plane brought in a whole bunch and we went down to help them sort/deliver it. I got a letter from Mom and Jean [my sister] but none from you. I guess I am being punished for you not having received any letters from me yet. By now you probably realize that I'll be writing quite often. If you can stand the philosophical vein, you should enjoy them. Well, Vern got two *Playboys*, and we have the foldouts posted up to raise our morale. Now all I need is that letter saying that you have finally heard from me. I don't like communicating with only one system—operating my transmitter, no receiver.

Well, love, keep your chin up and Brad's diapers, too. (Have you had any luck with potty training yet?) Because I'll be home shortly and you won't need a letter to know I love you.

Love, Gary

12. Bad News from Home

One of our great pastimes (second only to letters) was reading the local papers sent from our hometowns. My favorite, which I often read out loud to the amusement of my hootchmates, was the Hoxie, Kansas, *Sentinel*. Hoxie, the hometown of Murray Sloan, had a population of a few hundred, and it was a real trip to read about the trials of Mrs. Jones's lost cow, local meetings of the city council, and community issues—the daily trivia of a life we missed, so very different from ours now.

Just before Easter Sunday, Jimmy Martin was shocked to find an article about my son, Brad, in an El Paso, Texas, paper. Brad was recovering from surgery after being medivaced from Alamogordo. Jimmy tore out the article so I wouldn't see it because I hadn't mentioned anything about the event. I had no idea it had happened. My buddies told me they had had letters from home about it but didn't know any details and kept quiet because I didn't mention it.

I found out the facts when Carole's letters finally arrived. She and Brad were flown in a small military plane to El Paso when Brad choked on a chicken bone. Only the good work of our neighbor, who was a nurse, and our proximity to the local hospital (a few blocks) had saved him. He had a collapsed lung, but the oxygen he was given kept him going until reaching the El Paso hospital, which had a juvenile throat Roto-Rooter that cleared the obstruction.

Carole had not been allowed to call me. And she had arrived in El Paso with only the clothes on her back and had not found time to write. So I was the last one in my squadron to find out. Pilots are not the only ones who have close calls. I wanted to give medals to all who helped save my son.

10 April 66

Dear Wife and Son,

Easter Sunday, and I finally found out about Brad this afternoon at 2 p.m. when the mail came in. The stationery gave me the first clue, but I had no idea things could have been as bad as they were. Other people in the squadron have known about this for days—two at least—and none said a word to me, thank God. This morning Jimmy read the "El Paso Times" and saw the article, but he tore it out so I wouldn't see it since he knew that the last letter I had received from you was April second.

Sounds like super tot really gave you a scare, and I couldn't read your two letters fast enough to find out how my Son was going to come out in the end. God, I sure hope he is all right by now and there will be no lasting after effects. I hope you find the time to thank everyone who helped you and Brad. If it weren't for some wonderful people and machines, things would certainly have been bad for him. I'm just sorry that I could only find out a week later how close I came to losing my son.

I was going to write you and tell you that the best way to contact me in an emergency is the Red Cross—they have the best methods whenever I am overseas. I hope you don't have to use it ever, but you will know next time. Communications are real poor over here and its tough when the mail takes about a week.

We have been flying little the past three days, only sitting alert. So I only have seventeen missions total so far. We really don't know anything here about the revolts and demonstrations except from the week-old papers in the mail. Town has been off limits, and once again no ice. Happiness here is mail from home and cold drinks.

Major Vickery stopped by and he said a message is coming down on our forecasts for our next assignment. It states that those of us who wish to upgrade to the front seat on our return to the States will almost be assured of our being assigned to Europe in the front seat after upgrading, or else our base of choice in the States. So it looks like we can go to Europe if I survive over here and you and Son survive at home. I am going to try to get stationed over there. You can get started on the background work on selling our house so when I get more definite word you can put it on the market Also keep your ears open of RTU [replacement training unit] being started at Holloman, because before I go to Europe I will probably go through five months of upgrading either at MacDill or George TDY with you along. When I find out more for sure, you can get shots and a passport started on in

El Paso. The travel will be concurrent, so you and Brad can come with me as soon as I find a home. Being TDY for five months or so will give me five months on the housing list wherever I go.

Even if we have to sell the house without regaining some equity, if I can get things firm enough, we could let someone take over payments and you could have everything shipped to Omaha and stored. Then we could have a TDY shipment and a furnished apt. at RTU school.

If I can find out things far enough in advance we can make up what we would lose on the house by your going to Omaha and living with your parents. So, get your hopes up, as we will probably see Europe. Also let's get a nest egg started so we can enjoy it.

I am glad your mom came down to give you and Brad moral support. I'm sure it was very rough on you alone, and a shoulder to lean on helps when I happen to be thousands of miles away and a week behind in information. Growing up is a dangerous thing. I hope he will just have the usual broken arms, etc., from here on out since I'll get gray hair if this keeps up.

Well, it's late, and I have early alert duty tomorrow, so I will close. Please all of you be well and stay happy. My thoughts are with you and my love ever faithful. I'm thankful to have both of you two wonderful people in my life even if we are removed by a few thousand miles.

Love, Dad

13. The Officers' Club

We had little to do in our off time, so we took the opportunity to build an officers' club. The local engineers poured us a slab on a hill adjacent to our tents, overlooking the runway. Using poorly dried mahogany, nearly impossible to nail, we persisted in getting the building framed. But before we could nail on the plywood siding, the screen (for air conditioning), and the corrugated fiberglass roof, an afternoon thunderstorm blew the skeleton over to about a 30 degree angle from vertical.

"The f—ing club is crooked," Felix Fowler announced.

Not accepting this setback, we pulled two crew vans up and tied ropes from them to several places on the inclined skeleton. We reversed the trucks and pulled the frame close to plumb and vertical.

"The f—ing club is straight," Felix proclaimed.

Before it could lean again, we scurried to nail on the plywood siding. Then we untied the ropes. The club stood! It was still standing when we left the base. I suspect it eventually became a people's socialistic learning center after we Americans left haps it became a disco or nightclub after every the south was "re-educated."

ad a club, but no furniture. Felix sent our logistics offic... Rossmeisl, in the C-47 cargo plane assigned to our base to the Philippines to procure some. There were no official Air Force funds for this purpose, so Rossmeisl traded some huge cargo parachutes for rattan stuff. After a couple of trips we had a complete bar, rattan furniture, and even rattan chandeliers.

We now spent our off hours in the club. Eventually we got meal service and ate there instead of the mess hall.

19 April 66

Dear Wife and Son,

Your care package arrived today, and everyone on the street has been by to sample and look at it. It's unbelievable—a year's supply almost. We have already had some fudge and popcorn tonight and everyone is full.

I celebrated twenty missions last night in Col. Fowler's hootch next door. I can't remember how I got home. I just woke up at 0830 in the morning lying on top of the poncho that serves as my bedspread with all my flying clothes on. I never win in a drinking contest with majors. Don't worry about it becoming a habit, however. My head and stomach were so bad that I couldn't enjoy any of your care package until tonight.

You should see the club we are trying to build in a hurry. It is on a hilltop overlooking the base and we have all the unskilled men in the outfit working on it. The roof has been put together and taken apart three times now and we have just about torn apart and rebuilt everything we have done already. Our lumber isn't very good and tools are not the best—consequently, things aren't too plumb or square. This PM the framework was leaning to the north, so we took a truck and tied a rope to it and pulled the building (top) south. It is really funny watching a group of amateurs trying to drive nails. The skillful-coordinated fighter pilots can't hit a nail on the head. I even bashed my thumb the first day. We work on the club when we aren't flying, and there has been someone up there from eight in the morning until ten at night, every night for a week, but no outstanding results. I guess there is $20,000 worth of furniture waiting in the Philippines for us when it is completed. Gives us something to do on our off time, and it is not everywhere you can build your own club, you know.

No mail for two days now, as the system goes on as ever. I'll get down to the BX and get you a $3.00 slide viewer and mail it and the film to you sometime this month. Be sure and save those slides and keep track of them when you send them to relatives.

How much does Brad weigh now and how tall is he? Does he look like a "minimum pounder" and how does your figure look at 130 pounds? (Hint, send pics). I'm losing a little weight, but have a long way to go to look good. I love you two and would love to get a tape from you. I can use someone else's tape recorder if you could borrow one to send some tapes to me. Anyway, we will get going on that before the year is up.

Love, Gary

14. Club Bowling

After I was in Phan Rang a couple of months, air conditioned trailers were brought in and positioned down the hillside from the club, scattered so as to make poor mortar targets. They were assigned by rank, so lieutenants were last in line. Felix refused to move to a trailer until all of his pilots could have one. So the trailers filled up with staff pukes. We loved displaying our unit solidarity by staying in the hootches, and we despised the pukes. None of those "ground pounders" helped us build the club.

To reduce wind and dust, base engineers built a fence around the club using fired rocket pods. These empty aluminum tubes, about four feet long, could hold sixteen 2.75-inch rockets. We had a pile of them beside the club.

Some of the staff pukes took exception to our noisy club merriment. It ruined their air-conditioned sleep after a hard day's paperwork. We decided to retaliate. We rolled rocket pods from the top of the steep hill, scoring some direct hits on the trailers below. Once out of ammo, we joyfully returned to the club.

An irate major soon appeared, fresh from his shower, clad only in hat, bath towel, and flip-flops. He scanned the bar for culprits. We bowlers were hot, sweaty, and dusty. Naturally he confronted our youngest-looking, smallest lieutenant, Fred Frostic, who stood five feet six and looked about sixteen.

"Lieutenant," the major asked. "Were you the one rolling those CBU pods (the major did not know a rocket pod from a cluster bomb unit pod) down the hill?"

Fred, trained in the Academy's honor code, answered truthfully, "No, sir!"

The major then turned to Don Gordon, fellow graduate. "Don, have you seen any CBU pods up here?"

Don answered truthfully, "No."

Fred was one of the smartest guys from the Academy I encountered. He was constantly reading math books and doing equations in his spare time. We later flew together in Germany, where one day we were scheduled on a four-ship air-combat tactics mission. Two of the other birds aborted, leaving only us two. On the runway I called Fred on the radio.

"Give me ten seconds."

We had clean birds and no tanks. Having flown with Fred in Vietnam, I knew we could have a no-holds-barred dogfight. Fred gave me a ten-second head start. We never took the engines out of afterburner and never made it to the training area. We went eyeball to eyeball with lots of G-force on the aircraft. Flying the same plane, with equal skills, neither of us could gain the advantage. Seven and a half minutes later we had burned through most of the 12,800 pounds of fuel we carried and headed back to base. Fred was one of the few guys I trusted to play hard outside the usual rules.

On another flight in Germany I led the two of us on a simulated close air support mission over some Army tanks in a valley. We made low passes over the tanks, just clearing the ridge lines. We flew a loose tactical formation to and from the tanks, and when Fred rejoined in tight formation over Spangdahlem Air Base, I checked my wingman to be sure he was in tight. All the other pilots on base graded your formation, and if it was sloppy you caught a lot of shit. A tree branch was stuck in Fred's left leading edge flap. I radioed him to make a no-flap landing and check his left wing.

It's OK to brush trees in combat, but not during training. I think Fred got a poor mark in judgment on his next performance evaluation. As a result, he retired a full colonel instead of being promoted to general. Fred later became a chief strategist at the Pentagon and deputy assistant secretary of defense for requirements and plans. He was the only fighter pilot in the Clinton administration. His brainpower served our country with distinction, not to mention his service as a fighter pilot for twenty years. And he was a damn good bowler at Phan Rang.

15. The Lieutenant's Jeep

Transportation was one of our problems at Phan Rang. Each flight had one Econoline van—for eight pilots. It was about three miles to the flight line, so you walked or hitched rides when you could.

Our 101st Airborne officer-neighbors next door soon came over to enjoy our club. They brought jeeps. The Army seemed to have a lot of them, so we "borrowed" them from time to time. Military vehicles (including fighters) have no keys. After a few friendly thefts on our part, the paratroopers chained their steering wheels.

A few of us lieutenants believed that if Army lieutenant platoon leaders got to have jeeps, the government should provide a jeep for us. Not being greedy, we were even willing to share one. We formed a committee. Our new task was not to merely borrow a jeep, but to transfer one to the 389th for the duration of our tour.

Army jeeps are green; Air Force, blue. We lined up some blue paint and put in an order with our maintenance people for yellow numbering. Under cover of darkness we stole a chained jeep, which was able to make only left turns. It took many cuts of the steering wheel, backing, and turning to negotiate corners, but using our extreme piloting skills we succeeded in driving the jeep to our tent area.

The hootch next to mine was empty, so we knocked out a wall and garaged the jeep. At night we worked on its transformation, painting by hand. Felix visited often to have a beer and monitor progress. He liked his young officers' initiative and teamwork.

The Army, however, can't take a joke. They were obsessed with finding their jeep. They even sent helicopters out looking for it. We kept it covered with bamboo matting inside the hootch to hide it from Army search teams. Soon it would be blue and have USAF numbers. We lieutenants would have our own jeep for the rest of the war.

The 101st Airborne commander was a brigadier general; our wing commander, a full colonel. They had a conference about stolen jeeps. This wasn't good. Ultimatums were given.

Felix visited. Alas, we had to give the jeep back. That night a half-green, half-blue jeep divinely reappeared in front of the chapel. From then on every Army jeep arriving at our club had an armed private as a driver. No matter what the enticement—beer, food, or booze—he would not desert his post. Those Airborne guys were disciplined.

They would owe us a jeep, however, after a particularly hot, close-air-support mission we later flew for them.

16. The Missions

Each fighter squadron was composed of four flights: A, B, C, and D. A pilot generally flew as much as possible with his flight. This developed crucial teamwork. Our missions usually consisted of a flight of four, but two ships were often a single element.

Each day the primary flight flew twice. The same with the secondary flight. The tertiary flight usually flew once, maybe twice. The fourth flight, the duty flight, worked schedules, prepared target folders, and manned the phones and mobile control on the end of the runway.

Whenever we flew, one or two pilots manned mobile control. Pilots in a small glassed-in shack routinely monitored takeoffs and landings for safety. They were also there to serve as an extra pair of ears and eyes if a plane encountered battle damage or trouble. They were in radio contact with the incoming planes and the control tower and radar approach.

The F-4 was a versatile fighter-bomber. It carried air-to-air missiles, a 20 mm Gatling gun in a pod below the fuselage with twelve hundred rounds of ammunition. It could haul 17,000 pounds of ordnance—bombs from 250 to 2,000 pounds, napalm, rockets, cluster bombs, mines—you name it and the F-4 could carry it. (Later in Germany we sat ground alert with nuclear weapons. Our targets were behind the Iron Curtain.)

Our missions varied. We bombed enemy supplies, troop areas, and bunkers; prepared landing zones for helicopter assault by the Army; and impeded the Ho Chi Minh Trail in Laos and Vietnam, used by the North Vietnamese to supply their troops in the south.

Most of our missions had a forward air controller, or FAC. The FAC was a fighter pilot flying a light propeller-driven aircraft, carrying smoke rockets. The FAC usually flew with a South Vietnamese counterpart to help identify friendlies. FACs lived out in rough country, the boonies, operating from dirt strips. They flew their patrol areas every day and got good at noticing things the bad guys did to give themselves away. The usual procedure was to make radio contact over a target. Then the FAC marked the target with a rocket. He then adjusted our bomb deliveries, based on each individual bomb impact to destroy the target.

More and more frequently we flew close air support for troops engaged with the enemy on the ground. Close air became my favorite mission. In some cases we were in direct radio contact with our troops on the ground locked in a close firefight with the enemy. Our troops marked their position with smoke grenades using different colored smoke. We confirmed the smoke colors—red, yellow, green, or purple (goofy grape). Then the grunts on the ground told us what direction and distance from the smoke they wanted weapon impact. I soon learned to tell how hot an engagement was by the stress in the voice on the ground.

Our most accurate weapons were napalm and the 20 mm gun. We could lay both within ten meters of the friendly smoke, during frantic firefights on the ground. Unlike other missions, where you couldn't often determine if the enemy was there or what damage you caused, you got the immediate feedback and gratification of saving your comrades on the ground.

We flew aggressively into unfavorable terrain, in all kinds of marginal weather, to press a close air support attack, delivering napalm in a shallow dive, releasing it at a hundred feet above the ground, pulling out at about forty feet going 480 knots. In a similar maneuver we strafed, attacking ground targets with the 20 mm cannon.

In South Vietnam, enemy air defenses consisted of small arms and .50–caliber machine guns, not much of a threat to a Phantom aircraft hammering the enemy position. Flying so close to the ground was the real danger. Some of us would bring back leafy green souvenirs from missions.

Except for better radios and faster flight speeds, our ground support mission tactics had not changed since World War II.

One memorable close air support mission flown by our squadron was for the 101st Airborne. The paratroopers, operating in the highlands northwest of Pleiku, were in a terrible firefight and their position was being overrun. The company commander, Carpenter, was desperate. He requested napalm *on his position.* Ron Kovar led our mission. According to Ron, the flight dropped napalm dangerously close to the friendly smoke. They were splashing fiery napalm just down the ridge line from our hurting troops when Carpenter asked him "to drop it right on his smoke."

"I could not do that," Ron told me. "I got the pipper [gun sight] just over the ridge before I released." Carpenter, who had been the lonesome end on the West Point football team, received the Distinguished Service Cross for his valor during that battle.

I still think the 101st Airborne owed us a jeep for that.

Writing to my wife about my missions was a balancing act. I wanted to assure her that I was relatively safe, but there were dangers some of my comrades wouldn't write about. I cautioned my wife not to share what I divulged to her. She naturally was still concerned about our next assignment and possible further separation so difficult for a young bride.

9 April 66

Dear Wife, Son, and zoo,

What color is Buns and how big is he? Funny thing, I was just thinking the other day that if I was home, it would be fun to buy Brad a rabbit for Easter.

I guess I'll devote the first part of this letter to answering your questions. It takes about a week to get your letters or packages.

Now, about my missions over here. I can tell you just about anything I want. The only trouble is that some of the things I could tell you, the other guys don't want their wives to know for various reasons. Anyway, if you keep most of what I write to yourself or other disinterested third parties, then I can tell you much of what we are doing.

Every time we fly, we work with a forward air controller, for many reasons. He is in a little Cessna Birddog, or O1-E, the AF calls it. He flies over the same areas every day and knows where the good guys and where the bad guys are all the time. He, being low and slow, can see many targets we can't, such as bunkers, rice caches, and troops—usually they fire at him and he returns their fire with us. We go out on a frag order and rendezvous with a FAC at a certain point. We do not usually know what our target will be. Then we contact the FAC, who describes the target and marks it with a Willie Peter rocket (white phosphorous) then he tells us where to drop each bomb, can of napalm, or fire each rocket pod in relationship to our smoke and each other's explosions. Usually the targets are hidden in tall trees (the VC are dumb, not stupid) and we see very little except on napalm runs, which we make at 500 knots and 100 feet or so—then we can see a little of the target. We bomb bunkers for the Army and sometimes when they are receiving fire from the VC, we silence them. Sometimes the friendly troops are within 100 yards of the enemy so we have to be careful where we hit. Sometimes we hit known VC villages and then we can see hootches and buildings burn and explode. The FAC is our eyes and we are his swords. Often he can't see the target after we hit because of smoke and trees, but sometimes he can even see bodies lying on the ground. But this is rare. Because of the FAC, we are always sure we are dropping bombs on people who are shooting at us. But so far I have not seen any, and for that matter, if I ever get hit probably won't see it either.

They are shooting at us—as you can tell over the news every night by the planes shot down. We also have had a very few hits on our birds already, but they are very minor, so don't get yourself or anyone else worried about them. All of you girls should know that we are being shot at and shouldn't worry because you can't help us in any way, other than not getting upset. Generally in SVN there are no really classic targets such as tank convoys—troop areas or front lines—but wherever the VC mass together or stop to rest and reorganize or set up training camps and armories, etc., we soon find out about it. Groups as small as companies are kept on the move by ground forces, helicopters, and F-4s, etc.

Last week when the VC made the mistake of standing their ground against some of our troops somewhere, and they lost over 200 men from just two flights of jets called in to help. With the amount of airpower over here and the ground forces, maybe a few more, so we could occupy. The VC will be beaten, but as I said before we must win the people and they themselves must figure out how they are to live.

Now, I finally received two letters yesterday—the first from you since I had written you. They were great.

Yesterday while I was on the ramp sitting ground alert, I got to meet Danny Kaye. Sloan showed him the inertial set. He has his own Lear jet and flies, too!

I have two rolls of film to be developed into slides that I will mail to you so you can see what this place is like a little bit. Maybe when I go R and R I can call and talk on the phone. Today I am one-twelfth of the way through, and I'm hoping the next eleven-twelfths go as fast and smoothly.

23 April 66

Dear Wife and Son,

Well, tonight we finally opened our club. It isn't much but it is all we have. Things are rough, but we have freezers and drinks, but most of all we have lots of spirit. I have to fly tomorrow, so I couldn't get too "dingadow" (crazy drunk in Vietnamese). It's really great to be in a squadron with fighter pilots—none (a few) of the ground pounders on base helped us work on the club, but they all appeared on the hill tonight to open the club. We would have had a real blast if it weren't for the war tomorrow.

I didn't get to fly after all—additional sorties were programmed and a few scrambles today took all the airplanes we had, so no transition missions today.

Jimmy and I found out that we did good work on a flight earlier this month that we led. It was the one on the village that we told you about. The ground troops moved in shortly and counted the dead VC. I tell you this and I am sorry I did. I hope you realize what we must do and don't hate me for it. I hope my Son is never faced with war—it is not spectacular, interesting, etc., it is dirty, detestable, and cruel. But people like us here keep the cruelty and terror away from our friends and families in the U.S. People home have never experienced this and don't realize how lucky they are. People here have talked to Vietnamese whose fathers were killed eighteen years ago in the conflict over here. Believe me if the power seekers aren't stopped here or wherever else they seek to promote their rule—our nation will suffer. Please believe what I do and must do is right—not measured against an infinite or theoretical good, but the good that man must fashion for himself.

Enough of such talk. I'm sure that when I return to you and Brad, my life will return to normal with you, although I may be different inside. I will still be the husband you remembered last and the father Brad is yet to discover.

Love Gary

17. Route One Ambush

One morning we were on our way to a target northwest of Saigon when we got an emergency call: Anybody with any kind of ordnance near these coordinates come up frequency so and so. We did, and found an anxious FAC. An armored convoy had been ambushed on Route One out of Saigon. The lead tank hit a mine, the convoy was stopped, and the armored personnel carriers were taking rocket-propelled grenades from both sides. The troops abandoned their tracks and hunkered down in the ditches.

We made one turn, and there was the battle. Artillery rounds made impact on the east side of the road. We dove down on the west.

The FAC asked for the 500-pounders one hundred fifty feet from the road ditch (danger close). The FAC didn't even take the time to mark with smoke. We complied.

"Stop! Stop!" came the Army radio call. "The tree branches are killing us!"

The attack was broken. Squads of enemy retreated on paths. The Army had a Bell spotter chopper kicking out smoke grenades over them. The FAC could spot them fleeing and could adjust our runs on the smoke. We hit the retreating Viet Cong with napalm. This was a real shit fest—between us, artillery, and enemy .50–caliber anti-aircraft fire. Not to mention planes and helicopters flying everywhere.

As we made our passes, I wondered how many artillery rounds came down as we circled underneath them for our attacks. The radio chatter was unreal.

We asked if we could strafe. The FAC instructed us to hurry because he had more flights stacked up above us with heavier stuff to drop. We ran low on fuel and went back to base.

A few days later we read about the big battle in a Chicago paper. According to the story, the Army had cleverly detected the ambush and "prearranged air and artillery support." The "ambush of the ambushers" was set off when the "lead tank hit a mine." What a great battle plan! The only thing recognizable about the news account was the date and place. You can't trust a report from someone who isn't there. In fact, you can't be sure of any reports—not even mine. It's more than forty years old!

A few years later the FAC who'd directed sixteen air strikes in that battle was stationed with me in Germany and told me about that day. He was on the ground the day after, as the Army did its body count. This was the enemy's first big daylight ambush. The ground party found dead guys chained to quad .50–caliber anti-aircraft guns. So they meant business. The enemy body count was over one hundred.

That was the last big enemy attack in open country, in daylight, while the U.S. Air Force was there. If the weather was good we could concentrate too much firepower on them. The enemy, however, did own the night.

We never wanted to be in a fair fight, especially on the ground. Surviving was everything. That meant we wanted to have superior firepower. The enemy sometimes died so we could live. Our guys were the good guys, therefore the other guys must be the bad guys. But we had to admire their guts.

There is no glory in war. I took pride in saving our troops on the ground, but killing is a dirty business.

15 June 66

Dear Family,

Along with this letter, I'm mailing you a copy of the "7th A.F. News." It has a story about my front seat ride in the middle somewhere and a page behind it, a picture of Captain Martin getting some goodies from our wing commander. The article was pretty much what I told the reporter. I have had eight front seat rides now, and went on one this morning. My bombing is coming along swell—had a 30-footer and a "bull" this morning. That's not bad bombing at 500 mph, 4,500 feet above the target in a 45-degree dive from 12,000 feet. After awhile you develop an eye, like shooting a gun.

My AC and I helped save an ambushed convoy north of Saigon the other day. We scrambled and were the first jets there. A Vietnamese flight of A1Es arrived before us and one was shot down. We dropped six bombs and four cans of napalm and the VC started running from their ambush, so we caught some in the open with our guns. Forty-nine air strikes were eventually called in and the next morning the ground troops counted one hundred five bodies, but we probably killed over two hundred. They try to hide their losses.

There were tanks and APCs burning on the road, and the Army was really crying for help. They lost fifteen ARVN and thirteen U.S. troops, plus over a hundred wounded. So you can see we have some pretty fierce battles over here. We make the big difference with air power. After we arrived the VC could either stay and die or run. They did both.

It makes us feel real good to know we are helping our ground troops. That is the only time we "enjoy" our work. After being over here, I'm afraid I might change a little. It's a strange feeling to track through a gun sight, squeeze the trigger, and see high explosive incendiary cannon shells go off on the ground when there are people down there. Makes you realize how imperfect man still is. Well, we are all trying to do our job the best we can.

I am sure if you, and especially Bruce and Mike, could fly with me once and see the destruction, bomb craters, burning buildings, etc., you would know for certain that any sacrifice a few of us can make over here to keep such destruction from our own homes is worth it. When one gets away from the U.S. and realizes how nice we have it with our standard of living, one appreciates it so much more. I'm afraid some people I know will make me sick when I come home, but I sure want to come home and see you and Jeannie and family. I also want to make sure that Bruce and Mike don't believe in the glorification of war that you get from

T.V., radio, and newspapers. All these victories reported in the news cost us lives of young men.

I now have had several people I know personally shot down here, so I know war is no fun. Well, I didn't mean to get a sermon going or sound bloodthirsty, but I just want to be sure my family and friends understand a little more than what is on the news.

One thing I feel though—no one can tell me about God at home anymore. I've been closer to him on every mission here than anyone who's never been shot at. I hope that you at home, especially my two brothers, take time out from baseball and TV and try to understand what this is all about. Vietnamese boys the same age as Bruce and Mike are fighting over here. One statement I am afraid someone will make when I come home is, "I wish you would have killed all those bastards. We'll teach them democracy." I know some people think like that, but they have never had to kill anyone, so they don't know how it feels.

18. Front Seat

As the war escalated the USAF consumed both planes and pilots. All the GIBs wanted to become aircraft commanders. The upgrade program was an administrative black hole and required extending a combat tour in Vietnam or going back to the States.

The undefined program soon began for us. Lieutenants Day, Frostic, Winegar, and I were given five transition rides to master the front-seat functions of flying. We called them carrot rides because we might have had to pay the Air Force back by extending our combat tours.

Some of the older officers (we lieutenants considered old anyone over thirty) left the squadron, so the four of us were given nine rides on actual combat missions with real bombs and an instructor in the rear seat. This was not practice on a gunnery range. We got live targets, bad guys on the ground. It was as real as it gets.

On one of these missions I carried anti-personnel weapons—CBUs. This type of ordnance was delivered in level flight at two hundred feet above ground so the bomblets, dispensed from the rear of the CBU, had time to arm yet land accurately. I could select one or multiple tubes to eject with each release of the button. Desiring lots of practice, I selected single-tube dispensing so I could make more passes at the target. The other three aircraft in my flight selected multiple tubes, and after only four passes they were "Winchester" (the radio call for "out of ammo").

We worked with a FAC in a small propeller plane who had the enemy in sight. As my three flight members pulled up to watch me after dropping their own bomblets, the enemy was running from hedgerow to hedgerow to escape. They were pissed and shooting back—small arms and some .50–caliber machine guns. I saw a few tracers coming up.

I realized that perhaps it wasn't the smartest thing to be the only plane attacking, making me their only target. I made four more passes alone and gave them a bad day. The FAC thanked me for the extra effort. I joined up and our flight returned to base.

During my post-flight inspection of the plane for damage or mechanical problems, I found a bullet hole smack in the center of my left outboard wing section. It was the first time my plane had been hit. Sometimes you can be too aggressive, which I learned more about later in North Vietnam.

After those nine missions, we flew missions as aircraft commanders with regular GIBs. Now there could be no mistakes. We were responsible for sighting the target and dropping the bombs. Dealing with death directly was very personal.

We were excited, yes. We all were near the top of our pilot

training classes and chose fighters because we wanted to fly the airplane and make the decisions. From now on we four newly minted aircraft commanders would fly front seat or back seat, depending on the mission and crew availability. Two lieutenants would crew the world's best fighter. How good was that?

My first front-seat mission was on May 10. On the way to the target I felt confident I could do the job. Yet I prayed that my first mission with live bombs wouldn't involve close air support with troops on the ground. Thankfully it didn't, and I managed to get my bombs near the target. I hit South Vietnam successfully.

Carole remained concerned about my tour being extended. She also had a watch repairman make a pass at her. Lucky for him, I never made it back to Alamogordo.

21 May 66

Dear Wife and Son,

Got two tapes from you today, and they were wonderful—you even recorded them with the volume up. Only don't send me any more until I can get a recorder and send you some. I hate to borrow recorders from people all the time, so let's just write letters until I can either buy one here or you can send me one after I send you the money for it. I really do go through your letters and answer your questions. Perhaps you just forget which ones you asked several letters ago. I did take notes during your tape so I will run through them and make appropriate comments. I did receive your "loaf" care package and no one really cared for it—if you send anything else make it popcorn (quite popular) or tortillas and jalapeno bean dip. I don't need any vitamins yet.

The maids don't understand much English, but I bought a dictionary so I could learn some more of the language. As a gift for Mr. Baggett, how about a pipe or some nice smoking accessory? I get $208 a month and so far I've sent you almost $150 a month. I've got about $130 saved for Clark but I will send it to you if I get paid before I go. Your cheese made it here OK but don't send any more. It won't keep over here.

We have done no painting and the S.O.S. correspondence course is so bad that I hardly worked on it. Our flowers are growing good. We don't get flooded over here and there is lots of sunshine. The wash girls use soap—don't send any.

The pictures of Brad are very cute. I love them. It lets me see how he is growing into a little boy. Keep sending one or two every other letter or so. Did you really end his "boo" and is he really learning to potty good? That house-selling prospect was amazing. Maybe you can sell it without too much trouble. Glad to hear your bridge game is improving. I promise when I get home you won't have to worry about me getting upset about your bridge playing. What about the big storm in Alamogordo? I heard trailers were blown over. Your tapes were much better, and Brad still laughs the way he did when we used to play at home—sounds cute as ever. You know now that kids plus pencils, crayons, etc. plus walls equals a scrub job for Mom. It's traditional.

I told you this extension business was just to prepare us if something like that happened. There is nothing official about any extensions, so don't worry about it. I will keep you informed. You know that I am keeping a diary on my front seat rides only. I will even tell you about my third mission. It was about 20 miles SW of Saigon in a rice paddy area with hedgerows separating them. The FAC thought there were VC down there, so he fired a smoke rocket and they began to run from it and shoot at him. We then came in and dropped CBUs on them. After awhile the FAC would shoot another smoke rocket. The VC would run and shoot, and we would come in with our CBUs (level 200 feet). There were foxholes in each hedgerow, no houses or people near, and the FAC could count four of them that we killed for sure. We probably got more. I did OK getting the ordnance into the hedgerows, but was really jerky and spastic flying for some reason. Had a bad day. Anyway, a little jerkiness keeps them from shooting you down, so I'll worry about smoothness later.

Well, I just told you about a typical mission. We killed some people, and it doesn't sound very nice, does it? The only thing different was that I was in the front seat and my direct actions affected other people's lives directly and permanently. You won't want me to write you any more after this letter, which is good.

I'm sending you a slide that Ray Harmon took the other day. I'm smiling and don't look too bad. You know you can have prints made from slides real easily, so if you get any good ones, have prints made.

Just returned from watching "What's New Pussycat?" and it made me horny. If I come back to Alamogordo, I'll pay a visit to your watch repairman and fix his "clock" for him. Take good care of my Son, and your slim trim self. Also take some more pictures of yourself along with the little half pint. Running out of ink. (Got a new pen.) My hand is tiring and my neck is sore, so I quit with I love you in the morning, evening, afternoon, and all the time.

Gary

On June 27, 1966, Murray Sloan (Snake) drew the assignment as my first regular GIB. I worried he might be a little jealous, or possibly nervous to be with a new guy in the front, but he was delighted. He knew he too would get his turn to upgrade. I remember little about that mission, other than Murray laughing his ass off almost the entire time. I heard a lot of "shit hot" comments from him over the intercom.

Carole had written me about her stage role in *South Pacific* in Alamogordo.

27 June 66

Dear Hon and Son,

How is my 127-pound star of stage and sewing? I received my Father's Day gift today. As a matter of fact; I am wearing it now to get in the mood to write you. In addition, I received two letters also. One from Jeannie with a picture of Lori [my niece] and my family, and surprise! one from your Dad with pictures of you and Brad, which were tremendous. They caught you when you weren't posing, and that is when you are at your prettiest. The trunks are a little large for me (remember the PJs you sewed once?) but the shirt fits great. I've worn it up and down our street this PM and to the movie just to hear the comments. It's pretty loud, but no one believes that my wife sewed anything like this. Good job, hon. I'm also glad to hear you received my [birthday] flowers, and that you might have a buyer for the house. Now if I can get a letter telling me my boy is gaining weight, and is OK, and I'll really be happy. My morale was certainly boosted today, but I hope to get a letter from you tomorrow.

Speaking of tomorrow, guess what? Murray Sloan and I are flying together. That's right! Two Lts. flying together, no IP in the back seat. Just me as AC, and Murray as pilot. All the Lts. are excited about it, including both of us. Finally, after almost two years out of pilot training, I'm getting an airplane all my own. Keep your fingers crossed that everything goes well, no emergencies or ground fire to complicate the flight.

Those pictures of Brad climbing the fence are great. I know he is all boy, and it makes me feel there isn't anything seriously wrong with him. I hope so! Please love me as much as I love you both.

Love, Gary

Carole was very concerned about Brad's apparent malnutrition. We shared this worry during our entire separation. I felt guilty when I thought that my absence could be the psychological cause behind his lack of growth.

Murray Sloan went on to have a great career as a fighter pilot. He topped off his career as the aggressor squadron commander at the fighter weapons school in Nevada. He then made full colonel, was the director of operations of the 21st TFW, and later was the director of a highly classified program.

After the Air Force he flew for Southwest Airlines. FAA rules forced him to retire from the cockpit at the age of sixty, an arbitrary rule that makes no sense. Who in their right mind doesn't want their airline captain to have been a fighter pilot's pilot with thousands of hours' flying time in multiple types of fighters and thousands more in an airliner? I especially like to see grey hair in the cockpit whenever I fly commercial. You never know when that pilot might have to land his airliner in a river. If he does, you want him to have flown fighters first.

I would fly anywhere with Murray, even a Piper Cub to Alaska, but then we would argue about who sat in the back seat.

Since I've known Murray, he's been married to his high school sweetheart, Bonni. It takes two wonderful people to have a marriage that endures the frequent moves and separations common to a military career. Both grew up in Hoxie, Kansas, and possess the great values of small-town Midwesterners. They now live in Texas in an airpark. Murray still loves to fly and Bonni is his copilot. Their personal plane is in a hangar attached to their garage.

Murray tells a story about his first ride in my backseat. I had a bad day bombing (Was I nervous?) and the FAC asked me to go home. I don't remember it that way but must bow to Murray's superior credentials as a fighter pilot. I do, however, reserve the right to deny his version of my story whenever the two of us get together for drinks and 389th war stories with Bob Winegar, who now lives a few blocks from Murray. Poor Bonni! She sometimes has to endure the three of us at once. Carole, after forty-six years, usually retreats to the safety of a good book.

Larry Day, Fred Frostic, and Bob Winegar have front-seat stories, too. I asked each one of them to share one of their stories. Each provided me a first person account of one of their memorable missions. Here is Fred's story:

After our "practice bombing passes," two sorties on the island south of Phan Rang, I flew my first mission down in the delta with Bill Smith as my IP in the back. As we made contact with the FAC, he said, "Be careful today. There are friendlies within 500 meters." I asked Bill what to do and he said, "Be careful." It worked and I was the only one to hit the target on all four passes.

The other interesting sortie came after we "checked out." I was sitting alert with Don Burns. I had the napalm and gun bird—as lieutenants did. After dark the TACC [tactical air control center] called and said that the Army was in trouble up at Tuy Hoa and we were going to be scrambled. Don reminded them that napalm birds weren't supposed to be scrambled at night. They said "Stand by one" and immediately came back that this was serious stuff and we should scramble now.

I told Don that I hadn't had a night gunnery checkout. He said, "Come with me to the back of the trailer." When we did he said, "Here is your night briefing—do it like you do it during the day." So off we went. Gene Knudsen was in the back, breathing hard.

"Don't let me kill us," I said.

"I won't," he replied.

A C-47 dropped one flare, pretty dim, and we made four napalm and four strafe passes down a narrow valley where they were shooting from both sides. I found out a year later that no one was supposed to drop napalm below about a thousand feet AGL [above ground level] at night. There was a special God for us, I think.

Larry tells a story about the pressures a newly minted front-seater faced. None of us wanted to let down any of the lieutenants that would follow us, transitioning to the front seat. No matter what adversities we encountered, we had to measure up. Hiller "Twinks" McCartin, who was quite a character, was in his backseat.

I don't remember anything about my check ride except it was with Hawkins. The next ride was a two ship with the ops officer, Major Larry D. Welch [later to become the USAF Chief of Staff]. Welch was not known for his sense of humor, many words, or a laid back attitude. He was very serious and I was determined to put out my best effort. The mission was in the Delta with a FAC and we both had napalm and a gun. It was a little difficult to be too serious with Twinks in the back seat making wisecracks all the time.

The mission was uneventful until we started to strafe some small boats in a river. After my first pass we had utility hydraulic failure, which I dutifully announced to the flight leader. "Safe it up, climb to eight thousand feet, and start an orbit," was the clear and immediate instruction. After Major Welch joined on me and checked over my aircraft, he took the lead and we headed back to Phan Rang. En route he informed the Command Post and we were directed to expect to hold until some other squadron mates could land, as my landing would close the only runway with a barrier engagement. After everyone recovered, Major Welch asked for an airspeed check, told me to add five knots to my final approach airspeed, and reminded me to be sure I was not low or short on the approach. Then he went in and landed. Vern Womack's short landing had been a week or so prior and we were all being very careful and aware about where we touched down.

Twinks led me through the checklist and we made a textbook touchdown five hundred feet before the barrier and five hundred feet from the now graded end of the runway. The barrier grabbed us and we stopped in no time. As I was catching by breath and preparing to shut down an engine, I heard a lot of noise in my headset. I opened my canopy and asked Twinks if everything was OK but I didn't get an answer. I looked out the left side of the cockpit and there was Twinks standing on the runway after an emergency ground egress. He was frantically pointing at my nose gear. I could see a puddle of red hydraulic fluid. I thought we had a problem with the nose gear so I waited until the ground crew safed the nose gear before I shut down.

Further inspection revealed that I had shot off the bottom half of my radome and radar on my first strafe pass, causing the hydraulic failure. The gun barrel mounting bracket had failed so the barrel would wobble when it rotated, with every fifth or sixth bullet going through the bottom of the radome and radar. I couldn't see any of the damage from the cockpit. When asked, Major Welch said he didn't see any reason to mention the damage on our way back to the airfield, as it would not have changed any of our plans. The extra five knots on my final approach airspeed took care of it.

In January 1967 both Larry and I had flown all of our forty missions over North Vietnam and had orders for home. Our replacements were trained and we were given a break from Danang and sent to Clark AFB in the Philippines.

Clark scheduled us to fire a sparrow missile at a drone. We flipped a coin for the front seat on the first flight, then decided to alternate front and back seat rides. But the weather and living conditions at Clark were much better than Danang, so we thought we'd abort our first flight by contriving a "malfunction" and enjoy the day. The F-4 used hot bleed air from the engines to keep airflow over the wing and flap surfaces, allowing it to land at a lower speed. Valves in the wings closed when you raised the flaps. If they didn't close, you could burn a wing off, but the warning light in the cockpit rarely malfunctioned. We flew around the Philippines flaps down, sightseeing and burning off fuel. Of course the airplane ground-checked OK, so we had the rest of the day off. The poor maintenance guys had to ground check our "malfunctioning" BLC (boundary layer control) light.

We were rescheduled the next day, swapped positions, and lo and behold the same "malfunction" occurred. This attracted the attention of the Clark AFB chief of maintenance, a full colonel. He'd noticed that we were switching seats in the F-4 on every flight and became suspicious. On day three, as we sat in our bird, the colonel came up the boarding ladder and told us unless he saw a burning F-4 fall out of the sky, we had better get our missile off and mission completed. We got the message, flew, and fired our sparrow missile from 30,000 feet in a snap-up maneuver against a drone at 45,000 feet. One shot, one kill, but our vacation was over.

While we were enjoying our extra days at Clark, we were housed in trailers set up for aircrews to be used by Strategic Air Command for typhoon evacuation from another of our Pacific bases. When we checked into our trailer, women's underwear was draped on a line down the hallway. We had no idea who the owners were.

The second night in our trailer, at about four in the morning, we awoke to heavy pounding on the front door. Larry, sleeping in the room closest, opened it to find four air policemen on the porch. They insisted on searching the trailer for women. Evidently some former tenants had been cohabiting, and this was a raid to find the culprits. After a loud discussion, we were left in peace. We returned to the monsoons at Danang.

19. Johnson's Coffee Table

On one of my front-seat missions I made a mistake that I do admit to. It was the day Dick Johnson got a new coffee tabletop as a souvenir.

We had a flight of four with two planes carrying napalm, and two carrying 500-pound bombs. The FAC had a suspected troop concentration and supply area as the target, which consisted of several hootches and bunkers in the jungle. Enemy troops were thought not to be present, so the FAC elected to have the two planes carrying the bombs attack first, blowing things apart. Then the two of us with napalm would come in low and burn things up.

We delivered napalm in a 10 to 15 degree dive and "pickled" at a hundred feet, pulling out at about fifty. (The bomb button was called the pickle button, and I cannot tell you why!) So the two of us carrying napalm circled at altitude as the bombers made their first dives. Johnson was the lead, and he dove in.

"Holy shit!" the FAC called. "They have guns down there and are shooting."

Johnson agreed. He took two .50 caliber hits on his windscreen right in front of his gun sight (and eyeballs!) just as he released his bombs. He later sent the windscreen home and had it made into a coffee table.

Johnson's first bomb was a direct hit. All sorts of bad guys in black pajamas ran out of the hootches.

"Get the napalm on them," the FAC radioed.

Down I dove from altitude, but I hadn't turned up the defroster. As my cold airframe met the warm, humid air near the ground, my canopy fogged over completely. I hit full defrost and leveled out at two hundred feet on the radar altimeter, unable to see outside—*not* wise!

I called for heading vectors from the FAC. He gave me directions to the fleeing bad guys as I tried not to fly into the ground. Things were moving fast. Finally the defroster cleared a small spot on my front windscreen and I saw black objects on the ground. Bombs away! I pulled up hard, proud of my "expert" flying.

"Nice job," the FAC said. "You just wiped out a herd of water buffalo."

The flying was pretty damn good, but the decision-making piss poor. From then on I kept my defroster up whenever I was over a target. You never know what will happen. You can go from normal to puckered up and very busy in only a few moments.

20. Close to the Hills

When flying as close to the ground as we flew—at speeds up to 560 knots, which is about 950 feet per second—you had to learn to think ahead, otherwise known as staying ahead of the airplane.

The greatest danger in South Vietnam was not enemy ground fire but running into two-hundred-foot trees. I once rode through some treetops in the backseat with a new guy on his first strafing mission.

On one front-seat mission, our troops in contact with the enemy needed napalm close to their position. The safest run in heading for troops on the ground was laid out by the FAC: the grunts popped smoke, marking their position. I made my first run. I dove on the target, pulling out at about fifty feet, then started my 4-G pull out (four times the force of gravity). My windscreen was filled by the hills ahead.

I pulled back harder on the stick, reached the maximum angle of attack for the F-4, and held on. My GIB was hyperventilating in the backseat. I spotted a saddle in the ridge, kicked the rudder, and skidded over—luckily just clearing the hills. It was close. I remember trees above me on both sides of the plane. If that break in the ridgeline had not been there, I would have hit the ground.

My adrenaline was pumping. I asked the FAC if we could have a different run in heading because the hills were too close. From then on I was a lot more wary of the terrain beyond the target area.

I didn't write home about that one.

21. Close Air Support

Of all the missions we flew in South Vietnam, close air support of our ground troops was always the most rewarding. Like knights on horseback, who could charge in and often turn the tide of battle, we could break an enemy attack and save the lives of the grunts in the jungle. We had great admiration for these guys down in the jungle, eyeball to eyeball with the enemy for days at a time.

On one such mission somewhere northwest of Pleiku, a large enemy force had detected our long-range reconnaissance team, the Green Berets. Our guys were in a running gun battle and had fled to a point where the team was surrounded by a river on three sides. The enemy was pressing them from the fourth and the river trapped our troops. Helicopters had been called to pull them out of the fire.

Our guys were in deep shit. The question was, would the helicopters get there in time? As fate would have it, we were nearby flying to another intended target. We arrived first, laid a lot of fire across that finger of land, very close to our guys, broke the enemy attack, then strafed with our cannons as the team was plucked out of the river by the helicopters.

I knew for certain that day that we had saved some American lives.

I have since met more than one stranger who served in Vietnam as a grunt. Often, when I tell them I flew F-4s (known as Old Smokey by ground troops), I am treated to a free drink. Of course, then I have to reciprocate and listen to their tale. Every soldier has his own war story.

22. Loneliness, Sex, Temptation, and Wifely Worries

It was now July. We'd been away from our families for almost five months. Both Carole and I were feeling very lonely. Carole sold our home in Alamogordo and she and Brad moved back to our hometown of Bellevue, Nebraska.

Thanks to one of Colonel Fowler's schemes, I got a break from the war with an unofficial R and R trip to Bangkok with Martin. We had crew orders to fly to Thailand. We hitched a ride on a C-130, piloted by one of my training classmates. He couldn't get the gear up taking off from our base. We pleaded with him, so he kept the gear down and flew low and slow all the way so we could get to Bangkok.

Carole was distressed by continued reports of pilots being lost every day. Pictures of downed pilots appeared in the news, and I tried to make her realize being captured was a very bad outcome. My worries continued about my son as he underwent hospital tests for his lack of growth. I had some of my lowest moments at Phan

Rang, dreading the continued separation and facing the prospect of a much tougher war in North Vietnam.

2 July 66

Dear Wife and Son,

I'm astonished! I can't believe you performed an amazing feat such as selling our house in one day! You certainly must have been quite a salesman. I think you are wonderful and amazing. I hope you can find a good lawyer or real estate man to take care of the paperwork and legal matters. As soon as you get moved, I can get $130 dislocation allowance from here, and I'm mailing it to you. I want you to buy yourself a present with it, just for you. How do you really feel about leaving? Do you plan on staying in Omaha, and what do you plan to do there? I have so many questions—like where should I send my mail now, 2401 Main? And, most important, how is my boy? Those pictures you sent with your letter made him look skinny and pot-bellied. He does look like something is wrong. I wish I could be home to help you with all the paperwork details, but I have confidence in you. God, I wish I could give you a big squeeze right now. I 'm really getting homesick for you and Brad when I lay in bed and dream about you two before I fall asleep. I could almost cry. I love you both and miss you both so much.

One good thing about your moving. Now I 'm sure we can get together in Hawaii if I can just make it over there myself. Would you believe Sept or Oct? God, I wish this year would go faster or this war would end sooner. I need to be home now for both you and me and Brad. I can't hardly stand it and miss you both. Sometimes I actually have to try just to remember how you both look like. The pictures help but this separation has lasted too long already as far as I'm concerned.

Well, honey, my only orders for you are get my boy healthy and keep yourself busy and reasonably happy. You are free to go anywhere and do anything you wish. I know you will be very busy signing papers and finishing things up, but please let me know if there is anything I can do, and write me just a few lines any time you get a chance.

I'm sure your and my family will love having you by them so close. Don't feel obligated to them but remember it might be good you are there for we both may be overseas for three years or more, and all the time you spend with them is time you may not have later. I love you, you thing. I don't know what else to say.

Love, Gary

8 July 66

Dear Wife and Son,

I hope by now you are both alive after selling the house and moving. I'm sure it was quite a rush and both of you are tired from the trip and everything. You are getting better with that camera. Brad certainly does have a pot belly, and his ribs do stick out on that last series of pictures. You seem to have no aversion to taking snapshots in the nude of that boy. Speaking of snapshots, our flight is having a pin-up contest with our wives. Ray Harmon's wife is slightly ahead of Mrs. Larkan, but I haven't entered the race yet. I would like to see some more pictures of you all dressed up, or undressed. I must have sixty pictures of Brad and his mob, but only about four or five of you, and they are usually with a group of wives.

Yesterday I flew my thirteenth front-seat mission. Don Gordon was in my backseat and everything went OK as usual, although we had to fly in some very marginal weather, and we were bombing in mountains around Pleiku.

I'm very glad my Son has changed for the better, and I'm especially glad for you. I'm sorry I could not be around when he had you tired and irritable. I wish my shoulder had been there to cry on whenever you needed it. Your tears always make me love you, and I always want to squeeze you when you cry. I love you very much.

Gary

18 July 66

Dear Hon and Son,

Well, the vacation is over, and once again I'm in dusty, dirty, dingy Phan Rang. Getting away from here really makes this place seem miserable, but it was worth the trip just to enjoy living normally once again. I recovered from my first two days buying presents for everyone and managed to come home with fifty dollars in my pocket. I did spend $250 though, counting the $72 check. You and your parents should receive the airmail packages by the time this letter arrives. You ask where all my money is being saved over here. Well, trips like this wipe it out. I've only been getting about $200 a month, so I've been paid $800 since I've been here, and I sent $200 to you, and it cost me $60-$75 a month to eat and buy drinks at the club. If you count about $100 spent in the Philippines, and this Bangkok trip, you can see I have not saved a vast amount.

I admit I have been pretty self-indulgent on these trips, but I feel I deserve it. We don't get any dollars for these TDY trips, and a hotel costs about $6 a day, including laundry. Taxi $3 a day, guide fees to the temples $3, etc., etc. I even spent $8 one place for dinner and Thai dancing, everything authentic. We sat on the floor on cushions and had a real Thai meal and it was worth it. It sounds old, but I wish you could have been there to make it more enjoyable. Don't worry, though. I have four paydays before Oct. and will have $500 saved by then if I can get the R and R. There is still no word on it. So, I hope I explained where all my money is satisfactorily. I certainly haven't bought any fancy cameras or recorders etc. I am going to make you a long tape tomorrow and tell you more about my trip. I want to get this letter done tonight, so it will make the 0800 pick-up.

I really like those pictures of you. WOW! No wonder guys make passes at you—you're beautiful! Prettier than I remembered. I can't ever remember your having such good-looking legs. Wear some mini skirts and show them off. Those pictures sure make me want to come home. Send more! I hope none of your "serious" propositions have been vulgar and hope it is no one I know because I can guarantee you that if I see them when I come home there will be blood spilled. That's how I feel.

I haven't accepted any propositions either, and Bangkok is a severe test of one's moral fiber. Jimmy and I shared a double room, and we raised a few eyebrows at the hotel when we didn't take singles. All you have to do is have a single room and the girls will knock on your door. It took some doing, also the Thai girls are beautiful, but Jimmy and I took care of each other. Every bar and nightclub we visited had lots of girls, and I had offers from $6 to $10 "all day, all night." As a matter of fact our cab driver was amazed that we spent four nights without a girl. The way I see it is one night or several of purely physical fulfillment would ruin all the beautiful time we have made love and I will make love to you. (I get all tingly writing this even—that's how psychologically involved my loving you is.) Like you say, being away seems to make me love you more, and I have a beautiful marriage. I feel and I have a wife I can be proud of. Ask Jimmy Martin how many times I said, "Boy, I wish Carole was here, she loves etc, etc. It almost embarrasses me sometimes when I find myself talking about you to other guys in the squadron. Not many others ever seem to think as much of their wives, or seem unable to communicate with them like I can with you. I guess that's why they run around.

My favorite daydream-night dream is coming home to you and making love to you the first time again. Just like we were lovers or newlyweds. I've constructed it and reconstructed it in my mind a thousand times. When I think of the chance of being killed and never returning to you I hate my job, this war and civilizations that fight such wars. At times it almost brings tears to my eyes. I guess all this writing is my attempt to tell you how much I love you. Something that only can be done by coming home and living with you. I'm sure coming home means so much more to me than any bachelor over here. I am sure we are fortunate in a way to be apart, because not everyone can have a "new" marriage every year. It's damn tough being apart to do it though.

I'm glad to hear that Brad grew an inch and gained a little more than a pound. I'm sorry he has to be in the hospital, they are so rough on exuberant, innocent children who can't comprehend. I wish I could take some kind of extra punishment myself, and spare him all the pain caused by those that don't love him as much as you and I. I would give a million dollars to have him say, "Daddy plane" and run to me at the airport when I come home. I know it's too much to expect, but I want him to be conscious of my love for him. I hope he finally gets well and grows and grows so you have to buy him lots of clothes.

You need to send me copies of the orders moving you to Bellevue before I can collect your travel pay and dislocation allowance. If you don't have them, the transportation people at Offutt will help you get them. Also, I need to get your address change on my emergency data form. I'll use your name and my parent's address. Just let them know where you will be.

I wish I could have seen you and your figure in the play, "movie star." Do me a favor and stay sexy, but not too sexy. You don't expect me to leave you alone if other guys can't. Now I know I won't be able to when I come home.

I'm not flying in the front seat exclusively. I still fly with Jimmy mostly. I get a front seat ride when I can. It will be that way until some new pilots come over and I get one of my own. Actually, I'm really in a state of limbo, half front seat, half backseat—actually about 74%/16%. We had four ACs transferred to Ubon and Chritzberg and Lt. Murphy (backseat) sent TDY to Danang. Those going to Ubon will be home in Dec. (or dead, etc.), and those who go to Danang a month early. I would have volunteered for either one, but in my quasi AC state, I don't know what to do. Two more ACs are supposed to go to Danang this week. I don't want to go north as an AC, I haven't had all the necessary training or experience to cope with SAMS, MIGS, and flak simultaneously. We have two new ACs in our squadron and they just finished upgrading. The policy is not to send new ACs North for obvious reasons, and as a new AC—due mainly to native ability rather than to formal training—I and the rest of the upgrades here probably have less chance of going North than anyone in the squadron.

The thing is, honey, the situation here is changing, just as the war changes, and more people are getting 100 missions and going home. More replacements are needed here, etc. So, all I do is fly day by day. Each day bringing me closer to home. I'd like to go north and get home early, but as a new AC, couldn't fly up there etc. Also the flak is very thick and pilots bleed, including people I know, but they are doing a great job. It's pretty sickening to see the pictures of them being paraded through Hanoi, especially when I think I could be one of them very easily. Worrying about it doesn't do much good, however, so I don't.

Just use all your time keeping my boy healthy and happy. Who did you give Beau to? I felt bad you had to give him up, too. He had a personality at that. I also can feel how you felt about leaving our home.

I love you,
Gary

23. Korean Friends

Our neighbors the 101st Airborne kept most of the local enemy activity down to small-scale guerilla attacks. This was good because the only defense we had on the hill above our hootch area was a .50–caliber machine gun nest. We slept with our side arms close at hand.

Enemy activity started to escalate, however. They blew up our fuel pipeline from the coast, and it was even more dangerous to go to the beach for a swim. The bad guys were determined to prevent us having any fun.

With the increased threat, a battalion of Koreans came to dig in on our north perimeter, building bunkers deep underground. (It made us wonder about the quality of our sandbag bunkers sitting out in the open in front of our hootches.) These men were crack troops from their Tiger Division. It was the first time Korea had sent an armed force outside their country. Having been invaded for centuries by the Chinese and Japanese, the Koreans were extremely proud to be in Vietnam.

We soon met their officers at our club. A Captain Kim made me his special American friend, taking lots of pictures to send home. Kim, who spoke English, was the aide to the battalion commander, which meant he had a jeep. I got a lot of jeep rides.

One day, down by the 101st helicopter unit's short runway, two Korean privates were buying cokes from a local Vietnamese girl. It was funny watching two different Asians communicate, using pidgin English. Kim spotted the soldiers, jumped out of his jeep, and knocked them down. They popped back up to attention, only to be knocked down again. Tough outfit. Eager to fight, they took the offensive against the Vietcong, patrolling and engaging the enemy. We flew some close air support for them.

I learned more when Captain Kim invited me to train in Tae Kwan Do with his troops. I was six feet two and 205 pounds. The average Korean is about five nine and 165. I thought it wouldn't be a fair match. Naturally, being an American fighter pilot, I couldn't turn down the test. It was an "honor" to spar with their best guy. Most fighter pilots were not the toughest physical specimens, and I was no exception. I got the stuffing knocked out of me. But I had represented the flag. The next day I was sore and bruised. I managed to avoid future training with our allies.

My turn to train the Koreans came a few weeks later. Some genius got the idea that it'd be great for allied cooperation if the Korean battalion commander, a colonel, got a backseat ride in an F-4 on a close air support mission for his unit. Someone had to train him in ejection seat procedures, but his English skills were limited and I had no Korean at all. Since Kim was my buddy, I was chosen to explain and demonstrate procedures on the training seat to the two of them, then Kim would converse to the colonel in Korean.

The Martin–Baker ejection seat was a marvel. Rocket powered, it had zero–zero capability. While at a stop on the ground, if you ejected you fired into the air, the chute opened, you swung once, and you hit the ground safely . . . if everything went right. Unfortunately it's complicated by shoulder straps, leg harnesses, two eject handles, one handle to cut your straps for ground egress, one to fire only the canopy, and so on.

My three-way briefing was a nightmare. I could tell this wasn't going to hack it. This colonel was a reputed Medal of Honor winner in the Korean War, so if anything happened to him it wouldn't be good. On the way to the plane I had visions of him ejecting and my being transferred to a small island in the Pacific for the rest of my career. How did I get into these things?

As I stood on the F-4 wing, strapping the commander into his seat, I had an inspiration. I took his hands and placed them on his thighs. With a loud voice and emphatic gestures I told him not to move his hands or *zoom*, out he'd go! Captain Kim did his best to emphasize the *zoom!* I closed the canopy, gave the commander the sign of the cross, and jumped down from the wing. I could do nothing but wait and pray.

Thirty nervous minutes later, in came the flight of four. When they banked to pitch out and land, I saw that all the canopies were still intact. Thank the Lord! The engines shut down. I climbed up on the wing and opened the canopy. There sat the Korean commander, hands still on his thighs. He hadn't moved a muscle. Hot and sweaty, he had pulled Gs for the first time.

I asked Kim to ask the commander how it went. His translation: "It is more difficult than it looks from the ground."

24. Doughnut Dollies

Civilization arrived at Phan Rang! The Red Cross sent two social workers for the enlisted troops—one fairly good looking, one not so much—the only "round eye" (non-Asian) women among 2,500 men. We called them the doughnut dollies. They organized bingo games and other activities, all well attended.

They were housed in a trailer, surrounded by barbed wire, on top of the hill by the officers' club. A new regulation stopped us walking naked to the shower.

One night we had a reception for them at the officers' club. (Was this really a tablecloth, punch bowl, and silverware?) One of our guys, Critzberg, liable to do anything, infiltrated their trailer, spirited away a pair of panties, and hid them in the punch bowl. When the wing commander stepped up to receive the first dipper, a chagrined doughnut dolly ladled punch and panties into his glass. From then on a twenty-four-hour guard was posted at their trailer.

We didn't pay the women much attention. I think we generally felt we were better off without a female presence. When we weren't flying we liked things crude, irreverent, loud, chauvinistic, and unfettered. We didn't know anything about political correctness.

One night a second pair of doughnut dollies appeared at the club on their way to Cam Ranh Bay. Their C-130 landed with mechanical problems. Being new, they attracted a small crowd at the bar. One of the guys was particularly crude.

"That's OK," a dolly replied. "I've seen and heard everything over here." Tired of traveling all day, she added, "If I had a flight suit, I'd fly that plane myself."

A dapper bachelor, George "Ferd" White, was standing right behind her. He whipped off his flight suit and, completely naked except for boots and sunglasses, tapped her on the shoulder. When she turned, he handed it over. She hadn't seen *that* before.

28 August 66

Dear Heatherton,

How is my girl with the short hair? I got two letters from you today dated the twentieth and twenty-first, so it sometimes takes them a week to get over here. I am glad you have "jealous" thoughts about me and the girls at the club, especially when you don't hear from me for a while, because that is exactly the same way I feel when I don't hear from you for four or five days. I guess we both must be in love with someone. Anyway, you didn't have to worry about those girls. That picture of Brad and Stef [our dog] is cute. Stef really looked cute and Brad looked chubby, but on one of them you had more of Stef than Brad. I'm glad to hear that your gift finally arrived safely. I hope it was a little surprise after the guessing you were trying to do earlier. Sounds like Brad is really spoiling Grandma by letting her sleep with him, but it better not be habit forming. I don't want him inviting himself in the sack with us when I get home. But how did you knock yourself silly in the bathroom? Hope you just fell asleep and you don't do it again. The clipping you sent me and I'm returning as instructed, was a flight that I was on strange enough. It was close quarters because the friendlies were so close, but everyone did good work. I don't know what picture you saw in the "Bellevue Press," but my hair is cut real short right now, because it's easier to keep clean. Maybe I'll keep it that way when I come home. Speaking of coming home, you don't have to worry about me surprising you for a visit. There won't be any more such trips. Generals decided it was too big a loss of combat troops, so we stay here. Mom says she likes her bronze ware too, and she said Mike really enjoyed his fishing trip with you. Wish I could have gone along. We would have shared a midnight swim every night. "Thunderball" is on at the movie tonight, and I will see it the second time, I guess. I can't understand why I haven't received any "Bellevue Presses" as they were supposed to be sent the fifth of July—unless they are using the wrong address.

Sounds like you are getting ambitious again with projects. One time soon, we are going to move into a place and get some first class drapes. Don't worry about the boxes of junk. I'll help you throw things away when I come home.

We had a big "C" flight party at the club last night. Today was our duty day and my first day off all month. I'm going to have over 60 hours of flying time this month. Needles to say, we had a large group of happy drunks, and really enjoyed ourselves. You couldn't believe it if you were here. It was the first time in over two months that Vern, Jimmy and I had been high and we were all high at the same time. I really shouldn't tell you any details, but since you think I'm depressed I'll make an exception, but I hope you can appreciate the situation and realize how good it actually was to get drunk with the guys you go out and get shot at with everyday.

Well, we always roll the dice, so I drank free booze all night. It really is mayhem when everyone else clears out of "our" club. We started out on a campaign against tee shirts. Anyone wearing one had it ripped off. Col. Fowler lost his too, as a matter of fact; I got carried away and ripped half his shorts away too. We all had flight suits on. There have been smarter things to "campaign" against before; hats, survival knife pockets on flight suits, but tonight it was tee shirts. Doc Lee, our flight surgeon and Critzberg got fire extinguishers out and everyone got wet with water and drinks. Then we regrouped and mopped up the floor and swept away the glass, and had a contest—throwing people over the bar, plus our usual contest hitting each other in the upper back with a fist.

The most dramatic moment of the night came when, right in the middle of the mayhem, in walks a Red Cross girl on her way to Cam Ranh Bay from Saigon—the only girl in the place (really ugly, but quite unshakeable). Immediately, Jimmy and Vern came up to her and began to tell her that all the people throwing each other over the bar were good guys—she was safe from us, we were fighter jocks and "owned " the club. She said something about her travel difficulties and said she needed a flight suit or something to get to Cam Ranh Bay. George White (a bachelor) in the true cavalier spirit of a fighter jock immediately disrobed and gave the girl his flight suit off his back. Quite a gentleman. He proceeded to stand at the bar attired in sunglasses, combat boots, and his shorts as if everything was normal. A local Red Cross girl came in and took her fellow traveler down to a C-130 and George got his flight suit back. We all packed up a couple of hours later and went down to Sloan and Harmon's hootch and continued the party with some Army troops and a German cook for RMK, several civilians, etc. On the way we stole two jeeps and a staff car so our street was full of vehicles. Womack went to bed earlier, but we couldn't find him in our hootch, and found him wandering about wrapped in a sheet proclaiming to be "Lawrence of Poland." Several people threatened to give him a haircut, but I protected him. (So I was told.) Anyway, the party went on and finally the combatants began to drop from fatigue and exhaustion. The German cook found out that this was a party and ran off and got some cherry pie and dill pickles from his kitchen in the staff car. Some of our guys had stolen his jeep, which amazed him because he had the steering wheel chained. It would only make a one-quarter turn, but drunks are clever and they got it around corners by going forward, turning and backing up, and repeating the process many times. Amazing.

Well, I won't go on anymore, but I woke up in Bob Atkinson's bed (he was in Clark) at six am and went home. Jimmy went home and found two sandbags in his bed. They broke when he lifted them. So, to get the sand out, he used a broom and swept his bed rather than lift the sheet out.

Today we are all recovered without too gross hangovers and declared the party a success. As soon as we make it six months over here, we are going to have an over the hump party.

So there you are. Now you know our morale isn't too bad. I'm not depressed and was a happy drunk, as was everyone else involved. This might have sounded vulgar, childish, etc. (to some people it always would) but it was good. I'm telling you, but don't tell anyone else associated with the squadron.

Well, the movie starts soon so I'll sign off.

Love you much, Gary

25. Bomb the Wrong Country?

I had returned from a front-seat mission and shut down the engines when a staff car pulled up in front of my plane. It was the wing commander. That couldn't be good news. Wing commanders didn't make a habit of greeting returning lieutenants. Mine told me to get into the clean F-4 parked nearby, fly to Saigon, and report to the command post. So off I went, wondering what was going on.

At the command post I found seven of my squadron mates. Days earlier we'd been in a flight of four that attacked some bunkers on the Cambodian border northwest of Saigon. Our FAC told us that Army helicopters had gone in that morning and received heavy machine gun fire. We were to take out the bunkers with napalm so the Army could return. The FAC had a Vietnamese counterpart in his little bird who wanted us to hit two villages about a kilometer apart, but the FAC thought the westernmost village was in Cambodia. (Our government hadn't yet elected to hit enemy sanctuaries there.) Maps of the area were highly unreliable, and lots of strange stuff went on along the border.

After the Army incident some grey jeeps and trucks had pulled into the western village. The FAC told us to watch out for ground fire.

Our passes ran from east to west, pulling out over what the FAC thought was Cambodia. The FAC marked the bunkers with a smoke rocket and we made our first pass. One of our flight's napalm canisters hung up and got a late release, hitting somewhere between the villages. The rest of our flight's bombs hit the designated target.

We didn't know at the time that members of an international control commission had been driven to the westernmost village. Cambodians were telling them that the U.S. Army had attacked the eastern village, also Cambodian. When we commenced our attack, the commission members were walking between the villages. We didn't hit them, but I'm sure we scared the shit out of them.

I believe that the commission was Canadian, Indian, and Polish. A Warsaw reporter wrote an article about the group being "Attacked by American F-105s with rockets and bombs." (Another accurate news report!) Some U.S. State Department guy must have been assigned to read the Warsaw papers. This political hot potato got handed around Washington and ended up on the desk of General Westmoreland, commander of all U.S. forces in Vietnam. A note from Secretary of State Dean Rusk to General Westmoreland said, "Find out what the hell is up."

The eight of us, separated until our individual stories were told, had to plot each pass and bomb hit of the entire flight in detail to a room full of generals. Army and Navy big brass were everywhere, striving to prove that their units were not responsible.

That left us as the culprits. It took several hours. At about four a.m. the eight of us were put in a van and driven to Westmoreland's quarters, in case there were further questions. Several generals went in to brief him. We were left outside. The generals came back and told us to go home and keep our mouths shut. That was the end of the "Cambodia" story. No assignments to Antarctica. Just another reason I don't trust the news.

I had to remain tight-lipped when I wrote home.

5 August 66

Dear Hon and Son,

Well, mail came yesterday, and no letter from you, which is "number ten." I wasn't completely shut out though. Mom managed a one-page letter. She said you found a house and I'm glad if that is what you really want. I also suppose that you are busy moving, so you haven't had much time to write. I still don't know whom you gave Beau to. Don't you read my letters anymore? I'm not surprised you weren't too excited about those colorful bags I sent you because you were expecting something nice in the mail. I shipped it surface mail, and it will be a couple more weeks. Did you also get the registered package and the film I sent you?

Right now its raining—good thundershower type after a very hot afternoon. I haven't written you because I was in Saigon yesterday, quite unexpectedly. Jimmy and I had to brief some generals on a mission we led, which you probably read about in the papers, but I can't say any more than that.

We stayed at one of the GI hotels in Saigon. One of those with the wire screen all over the front and cement barricades to prevent VC bombers from getting close with their explosives. It was really a raunchy hotel. Lizards all over the walls, and we didn't have any lights in our room, so we had to use a kerosene lamp. In the morning there was no hot water or light in the bathroom. That early morning Saigon traffic is really murder, with bicycles and scooters all over the place. The entire city is nothing but a series of bunkers and guard posts and barbed wire. I don't care if I ever go back there again.

I hope you have found a nice place to live, and that you also find that life at home isn't too unpleasant and that Brad is getting along well. How about sending me some of those pictures I'm always asking for, plus a progress report on how Brad is growing? How tall is he and how much does he weigh? Then, how "big" you are and how much you miss me. I really miss you and love you both. I just hope I can come home to both of you and make up for a year of loving that I can only write about now.

Love, Gary

P.S. Here are a couple of goodies to sweeten the pot. Buy yourself something nice.

26. Flames at Phan Rang

One day, about noon, those of us not flying were having lunch in the officers' club, watching activity on the runway from our high vantage point. Suddenly an F-4 aborted takeoff and caught fire. A *big* fire!

The base fire chopper flew out and dropped its fire-suppression bottle. The flames initially diminished but burst out again. Down the airfield sped a fire rig, charging across the infield, lights flashing, dust churning, closely followed by a staff car. But there was a ditch about ten feet deep in the middle of the airfield, perpendicular to the runway. *Bam!* In went the fire rig. Blinded by the dust, the colonel racing in hot pursuit landed his car right on top of the fire rig, ending all fire department activity.

Napalm augmented the flames and 20 mm cannon shells discharged. The F-4 burnt right through the aluminum runway. *Who the hell was in that plane?* we wondered.

That evening at the bar we heard the story. Charlie Hall (AC) and Ferd White (his GIB) had a brake lock up on takeoff. Before they could stop the 60,000-pound plane, the brake had overheated and caught fire. Soon the wing was fully engulfed, lighting fuel in the wing and the magnesium strut as well. Charlie and Ferd did a rapid ground egress, pulling the guillotine handle on the ejection seat that cut all their shoulder, lap, and leg harnesses. Ferd, not having to shut down the engines, got out first, bailing over the side and running from the plane. (Ferd was no dummy.) He turned to look back and saw Charlie hanging upside down, just above the ground, dangling helplessly over the side of the flaming airplane. His leg restraint strap had not released and trapped him. Flames were everywhere.

Ferd ran back, pulled the big knife we all carried on the calf of our G-suits, and cut Charlie down. Both ran like hell as the napalm and cannon rounds went off.

Charlie ended up with a knot on his head after Ferd cut him down. Ferd was burned on one arm. Otherwise both were not hurt.

We thanked them for the spectacular show. One plane was lost, but no pilots. One fire truck and staff car were out of commission. And the runway was closed for repairs, so our missions for the next day were canceled. This called for a big party. Hall bought Ferd plenty of drinks.

27. Safety Demonstration

Once a week Verne Womack, our squadron safety officer, briefed us on staying safe. He was competent and serious about his extra duty.

The engineers had built a huge concrete lip on each end of our aluminum runway to keep it from sliding around when overrun by a 60,000-pound aircraft. The lips and runway stuck up about two feet above the surrounding terrain. The runway also had a single cable across each end, about one thousand feet from the approach. The F-4, originally designed for the Navy, was equipped with a tail hook. A mechanical device attached to the cable allowed the pilot to snag it with his tail hook and slow the plane from 150 miles per hour to zero in about 150 feet. It came in handy if you had a brake problem, hydraulic failure, or other worry about stopping.

One particular day Verne warned us about the concrete lip, and to be careful not to land short and hit it with our wheels.

That day Verne and Don Gordon (Gordo) lost utility hydraulic power (their brakes and stuff). Verne chose to make an approach end barrier engagement with his tail hook. Down went the hook and in they came. They landed about two feet short and their landing gear hit the concrete lip. Off came the wheels, struts, and the right wing wraps over the fuselage. Verne's F-4 continued down the runway on its belly, sparks flying. No one was hurt, but another $2.5 million F-4 was ruined—and the enemy was not responsible for the loss. War was expensive.

We decided unanimously that Verne's safety briefings were bad luck. Each time he started one we booed and hissed.

Those damn engineers should have sloped the dirt in front of the runway. This accident could not be pilot error.

28. First Casualty

Late one September afternoon, word spread that a bird was down close to base. The rescue chopper went out. John Critzberg, AC, came back. Gene Knudsen, GIB, didn't.

The F-4's Martin–Baker ejection seat was designed to eject safely with zero altitude and zero airspeed. The sequence was rear seat first, avoiding the rocket blast that came back from the front seat. Gene probably got out first. At low altitude, when he ejected, he had no time to steer his parachute. He landed in the fireball and wreckage of a fully fueled F-4.

Everybody was shaken. None of us ever talked about buying the farm. We wanted to believe we were invulnerable and that it would take a golden BB to shoot us down. Now we knew better. What we did, sometimes twice a day, was dangerous.

We gathered that night at the officers' club. Felix, in his own true fashion, said, "OK, boys. A moment of silence." Then he lifted his glass. "Now let's drink to Gene." And afterward, "OK, let's get on with it." That was our memorial service for Gene.

Felix cut squadron orders (counterfeit for travel to the States) and Bob Winegar, my best friend and an Academy graduate, escorted Gene's remains home. The memorial service was held at the Air Force Academy.

Next to meeting loved ones at a fallen warrior's funeral, the saddest job a pilot ever has is going through that comrade's footlocker, deciding what to send home to his loved ones. The footlocker holds the most cherished reminders of loved ones left behind.

We had been gone from home six long months, and both wives and warriors were trying to weather the long separation. I had a hard time telling Carole about Gene's death.

15 Sept 66

Dear Wife and Son,

Finally, after six months, I'm writing a letter with a real ink pen. The BX finally got some refills in so I'm getting Uncle Sam's ballpoints when I write to you. I'm sorry to hear you are so depressed over another six months' separation. I guess I wrote you too much about reaching the halfway point and being home, etc.

I won't be getting an R and R slot to Hawaii next month. I still could possibly make it over there through devious methods, but I would have no assurance of transportation there, or back to S.V.N. especially since MACV has specifically stated a policy of only R and R trips to Hawaii, no leave. So, I think it's too great a risk to take. I'd hate like hell to have you over there and me unable to make it to see you. So, you probably ought to forget seeing me until sometime later, maybe not until next March. I know you will be disappointed and so am I, but we are on the downhill side. I hate to get letters from you when you are depressed. I am as lonely as you, and it is tough over here in many ways. I want you to perk up, get active and be the Carole I knew six months ago. Where is that wheeler-dealer I used to know? What about some projects and things? I know nothing is a good substitute for a husband, but you made it through six months OK, so the next six should be easy because you know there are not six more after that.

I am sorry you haven't heard from me for four days. I have been writing pretty regularly, except for the past few days. Did you airmail my socks? Surface mail takes too long. I will be home before anything can reach me pretty soon. Honey, I love you and I hope my memory is not fading. I am real and alive, and I am not near you now, but I love you just as much. My only means of showing you is my letters. I bought you and Brad each a gift today, and will mail it as soon as I can get down to the APO—airmail it too! I want you to send me your telephone number so I might call you if I ever get near a telephone again. Please write and let me know if you're seeing me in Hawaii is really that necessary to you. The money involved does not mean much to me either. If I don't see you in Hawaii, we will spend it when I get home, I am sure. The chances are just too great outside of an R and R trip of my not getting to see you, and think how bad you would feel to be there if I couldn't make it. Please write me, because your last letters make me feel you are getting despondent and the loneliness is getting to be too much. I hope not. Stefans are made of stronger stuff than that. I am going to start worrying about you more than I do about Brad not growing. I do think about you both a lot. You don't know how much I worry when I don't get a letter from you for four days. I have all kind of jealous thoughts, especially after you write me about seeing some old flames.

Now for some bad news. I wrote you about it last night, but could not mail the letter. I still am not sure I should tell you, but you would probably find out anyway. We lost our first squadron member over here. Gene Knudsen went in with the bird on join up just after takeoff. Critzberg was in the front seat and barely ejected in time himself. He landed in a tree and is OK. Gene was making the join up and the aircraft went out of control. We don't know why, and probably will not ever find out for sure, because everything was almost completely destroyed in the crash. Critz tried to get the bird under control, but it rolled over on him and the nose pitched down. They were low to the ground. He said "Eject" and thought he heard Gene leave the airplane, but they found him in the wreckage.

We all more or less expected it to happen sooner or later, but it is tough to find someone you know will be with you no more. Our job is a little more dangerous, but we have to live with it. Now, I want you to accept it. People die all the time, and before you and I both die, many people we know will have died, including our parents. Maybe dying is good. I don't know what I believe about it—just that I don't know. Keep yourself from worrying about it too much, hon. I am sure you too were expecting to hear such from me before the year was up.

Now, about my boy. He is really getting to be something, it sounds. I just hope everyone does not scare him about

Daddy coming home and shaping him up. I am going to love him and probably spoil him more than anyone ever has when I get home. I just hope he is not scared of me when I do get home to see him. I hope he starts growing too. Is he above the absolute minimum size for his age yet? I cannot believe that Lorri is taller than he is and six months younger. I am sure I will get him to eat when I get home.

Have you been motorcycling? I know it was probably a futile gesture to send that letter to Bruce and Mike. I have not heard any word from home about it from anyone. I know too that Dad is very sensitive about criticism, and I am not a world authority on teenagers now, but I am still glad that I wrote. I will do better when I get home, I am sure. Letters are a hell of a way to communicate.

I wish I could talk to you now, there is so much I need to say to you, hon. I have finished "Armageddon"—great book! You are in your "Armageddon" now. So am I, I guess? I love you much, hon. That is all I seem to say in my letters. You are my funny nose, and honey bunch of stinking weeds, even if the midget monster does say, "Momma nuts." I love you.

Gary

29. My Closest Call

Over a two-week period, three aircraft hit trees and lost windscreens. It took forty-eight hours to cure a replacement and we were out of spares. Naturally we received a briefing not to break any more windscreens.

I flew number four in a flight of four. The newest guy always got to be "blue four." Our targets were enemy bunkers. We dropped our heavy ordnance and uncovered the bunkers. Then we went in to strafe with our 20 mm cannon. We strafed at two hundred feet above the ground, in a slight dive.

Hung on the centerline of the F-4 was a Gatling gun pod that fired six thousand rounds per minute. The gun was bore-sighted to shoot through the "pipper" [gun sight] at 1,600 feet. It was mounted so that the cannon shell's trajectory moved through an initial upward arc at a range of 1,600 feet, then fell through the sight line again at 1,200 feet from the target. If you fired between 1,600 and 1,200 feet, the rounds went right where you had the sight. Once you fired the gun and the rounds exploded on the target, you could aim the gun like a garden hose and walk the rounds where you wanted. With practice every day, we became extremely accurate.

That day I could really see the bunkers. I came in and fired, got greedy, and tapped the rudders moving the nose and the gun so I could hose them all. *Boom!* I got a terrific secondary explosion from the ammo stored in the bunkers. A big fireball and lots of logs and debris blew up right in my face. I had no time to react. *Bump!*

The airplane shook as I pulled out. My master caution-light panel inside the cockpit lit up like a Christmas tree. As I circled to the left, following my three other flight members, I was in a constant turn and busy checking my systems and gauges in the cockpit, occasionally glancing out the side of the canopy to stay clear of the three aircraft ahead of me as they wheeled around for another strafing run. Some of the warning lights went out, so I decided to attack again. I rolled out on target, looked up through my center windscreen, and could not see out! The windscreen was shattered.

There were no friendlies around, so I could safely shoot without the gun sight. All I had to do was point the nose of my plane in the general vicinity of the target. So I hit the trigger. No gun!

I pulled off the target and climbed for home. I asked my element lead to come look me over. I was losing hydraulic pressure on one flight control system and had more warning lights come on when I put Gs on the plane to pull out. My wingman closed up underneath and, as he maneuvered closely below, gave me a running commentary on the damage.

I needed to get back to base. On the way I lost one flight control hydraulic system and my utility hydraulic system failed, which operated the brakes, landing gear, flaps, etc. If I lost the one remaining flight control hydraulics, I would have to bail out, hide from the bad guys on the ground, and hope a helicopter picked me up. If I made it back to base, with no brakes I would have to drop the tail hook and catch a cable across the runway. Thankfully, after Womack's safety demonstration, the lip on the edge of the runway had been graded to runway level.

I made it, but fuel was short. I declared an emergency and all the fire trucks were waiting for me. I had to blow the gear down with an emergency air bottle. I made the barrier engagement, shut down the engine, and had a tug come out and tow me in. The plane was a wreck.

The wing commander saw my shattered windscreen and shook his head. It would be some time before that plane flew again.

I flew the next day and tried to be more careful. I didn't write to Carole about it.

30. One Long Day

One day, after I flew two scheduled missions, I went out late with Jimmy Martin, my AC, to the alert shack to sit watch at the end of the runway until morning. We had just put our helmets and gear in the alert birds when we got scrambled. Had it been five minutes earlier, the crews we had just relieved would have flown.

A Green Beret camp north of us was being attacked. It was growing dark in mountainous terrain and there were low clouds. We had difficulty getting in under the clouds, finding the target location, and not hitting the ground. We made it in, turned around, rearmed, and went a second time. This time it was pitch black, making it even harder to cope with the weather and terrain. The Army was firing flares to light the battlefield. This camp was in real trouble.

Because of the weather we were the only guys who knew the way in through the mountains. We made two hairy trips in the dark, the last one after midnight.

Ray Harmon, who flew wing that night, deserved a medal. His plane lost its stability augmentation system, which was a computer assist that kept the aircraft stable. Without it the F-4 was a real handful to fly. It never went where you wanted it to, so you were really busy at the stick. Ray could have grounded his plane, but he went anyway. This exemplifies again how much we did to help ground troops in trouble. None of us wanted medals for that night. But we badly needed sleep. It would have been unsafe to fly again.

I seemed to be a robot, putting in missions and trying not to think about the job. The danger had become normal, and my letters about it casual. But both of us were missing the physical part of our marriage and dreading the next six months.

5 Sept 66

Hi!

I too haven't written for a couple of days, but I have been too busy. I spent yesterday on alert and flew twice the day before. I actually got up at five a.m. one day, flew four times—two day, two night—and finally finished up at two a.m. the following morning, twenty-one hours on the job. I ended up flying seven times in thirty-six hours, and have ten missions this month already.

Today, I flew in the back seat with a new guy from an RTU at George, and he manages to hit a tree on one of our strafing passes. No real damage, just a few wood chips in the intakes, but it makes me wish I was up front, because I can do better. I get $65 per month for riding front or back over here. I'm also scheduled twice tomorrow. So, I have a good excuse for not writing these past two days.

I'm putting in for my R and R request tomorrow, but something may prevent me from going as expected. I can't tell you what it is because we don't know for sure, so keep your fingers crossed. We could use the money in the bank anyway. If you have some spare money, save it. McDonnell Aircraft stock just split and now is a good time to buy. We don't get in trouble from "drunks" at the club because we are the combat troops. The officers do almost all of the fighting in the Air Force. We deserve a good time once in a while. And not many airmen see us anyway. Enough pressure does build up that it can and does become necessary to release it, and don't let any ground-pounders interfere.

It's getting real tough being away from you. I've spent about the past week dreaming and thinking about you and it's really bothered me—I'm so horny lately it's bad. I'm working hard so that helps, but this next six months are going to be rougher than I thought. I'm glad you admitted needing some loving. That is good. You can't be too sexy, feminine, or sensual for me when I get home. You can count on me being "animal" for about a month at least. Your writer's school and books arrived finally, so did the Bellevue Press—surface mail number 10! Just don't call up any of your old boyfriends. I'm jealous you know.

That tape you sent me makes me sad. You are very lucky you have Brad. It must be great having him grow up before your very eyes. I find it hard to believe that my boy will be able to talk to me when I come home and I'll be able to teach him things and learn with him. It's terrible being away. Sometimes I wish I could forget about you both, but almost constantly I think of how much I love you and want you again and how much pleasure it will be to see my son and hold him. It really tears me up when I have black thoughts and think of the danger here and my chances of not coming back to both of you.

Luckily, most of the time fear and such thoughts are subconscious, but there are some missions that give me a dry throat and a tense grip on the throttles through sweat-soaked gloves. Thank God it usually is only for a few minutes at most on any mission. I can't really describe it, and sometimes I can't even logically think about being over here. I'm just here and the things I'm doing just seem to happen. There is little outside world to connect things with. That is why I love your letters. They make me feel things from the outside world. I love you for it and I doubt I could exist without them. I can notice that my morale is really affected by my mail from you. If I go over two days without a letter, I can imagine all kinds of reasons for you not writing. I just hope that when I come home, we can talk and love and do simple things. Take walks in the woods with Brad and be alone together. I don't care if I talk to anyone else or even see them. I feel that I am a person that feels things deeply and my love for you is something almost alive within me. I don't seem to find many people to really talk to seriously. No one really wants to think about this war. It is hard to do if you are in it, because you have many thoughts and there are many ways to think of it.

This year of being pen pals instead of lovers is hard, but I really feel my love for you has grown. Maybe not grown, just that I've become more aware of it and really how much more a man I am because I have you to love and my boy too. I am so much more because of you. If you were in my arms now, you would know because I'd hug you hard and long, and you could feel my love in my grasp. Damn, I'm coming home so you don't have to read letters as the only way to know I love you.

Love, Gary

Author in Alaska

Fred Frostic

Felix Fowler, Sq. Commander

Major Bob Vickery

Bob Atkinson

Phan Rang Ops Tent (photo by Larry Day)

Phan Rang Hootch

389th Gunships

Phan Rang Hootch Area

Phan Rang Mess Hall

Phan Rang O Club

Martin Mortar Drill

Gordon Womack

Larry Day Squadron Ops Area Phan Rang (photo by Day)

Fred Frostic (photo by Frostic)

Ray Harmon, Mick Larkan and Verne Womack

Drury Callahan

Author in Phan Rang

Dick Johnson

Gene Quick

Danang

Danang Wing Ops

Danag 389th Ops

Doom Club (photo by R. Winegar)

389th Barracks Danang (photo by R. Winegar)

Doom Club Trophies Frostic and Others (photo by R. Hamilton)

Bob Winegar (photo by Winegar)

Ed Montgomery (photo by Montogomery)

Bob Wickman (photo by Wickman)

Author with 500 pounders

Murry Sloan and Bob Winegar

Willie Rudd

Ferd White

Hiller McCartin

BOOK THREE:
BATTLE IN NORTH VIETNAM

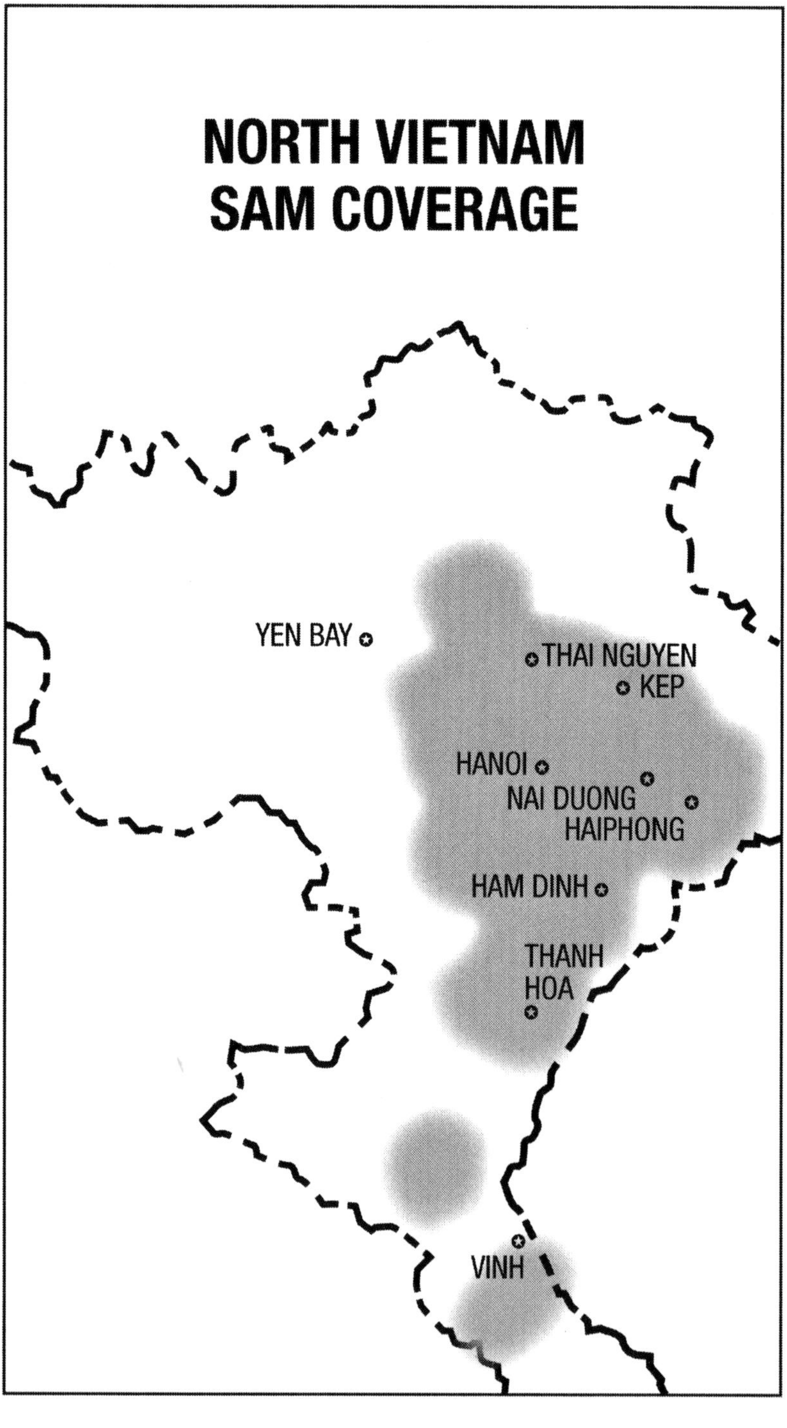
NORTH VIETNAM
SAM COVERAGE
YEN BAY
THAI NGUYEN
KEP
HANOI
NAI DUONG
HAIPHONG
HAM DINH
THANH
HOA
VINH

31. Danang—October 1966

The fun stuff was over.

In our six months in South Vietnam and southern Laos we'd destroyed three of our own aircraft, along with one fire truck and one staff car. Our previous ground attack missions, facing only enemy small arms and machine gun fire, were relatively safe. We lost only one of our comrades (but still carried that loss with us).

The war over North Vietnam had been carried on the shoulders of the F-105 (Thud) drivers, based in Thailand, and the Navy operating carriers in the Gulf of Tonkin. Now our F-4s joined the fray. Operation Rolling Thunder gained momentum. The "brains" in Washington were escalating the war.

Our entire wing was reunited at Danang. Our four squadrons bombed targets in North Vietnam twenty-four hours a day. We went deep into North Vietnam to hit targets around Hanoi. In addition to small arms and machine gun fire, we saw heavy anti-aircraft guns, surface-to-air missiles (SAMs), and, what we all hoped for, enemy MIG fighters.

It was monsoon season. Thirty inches of rain a month kept our flight suits damp, even when hung indoors to dry. Our leather grew mold and metal corroded. The weather was sometimes a bigger a factor to deal with than the enemy.

Our twenty-four-hour flight schedule had squadrons rotating between day and night shifts. Our call signs were desert animals, since we came from the New Mexico desert. Whenever a coyote or roadrunner flight was in trouble, it was one of ours.

Danang had two runways and was at times the busiest airport in the world. It was also the main U.S. Marine base. Marines were dug in all around, and the enemy surrounded us all. At night the local barber might don black pajamas and send mortar rounds crashing into the base, then return the next morning to be paid for GI haircuts.

We no longer lived in hootches but in a guarded compound, corralled by a barbed wire fence, within the base perimeter. A narrow, potholed macadam road circled our four squadron buildings, the theatre, and a field mess we named the Doom Club (Danang Officers' Open Mess). A bunker with steel planking and sandbags on top sat outside each building.

The two-story masonry barracks were originally built by the French. They had fifty-cycle electricity, an open bay area with bunks, and an enclosed shower. A dead lizard greeted us in the shower. It took two weeks before someone removed him.

Almost every night we endured enemy probes and attacks. With incoming fire, Marine outgoing fire, flares, and our occasional bombing on the perimeter, each night at Danang was like a giant war movie, again without popcorn.

The town was usually off limits, but for some reason our base exchange (BX) was located two blocks outside the base gate. One morning, needing toothpaste, I loitered at the gate armed with my .45 pistol until I saw three Marine privates in helmets and flak jackets, armed with M-14 rifles, heading to the BX. I liked the additional weaponry and fell into step with them. About a block from the BX, a blast of automatic weapons fire opened up ahead. I decided I didn't need the toothpaste after all and went back to the gate. The Marines shrugged and continued on.

12 Oct 66

Dear Wife,

Well, I'm here. I hope it will be just for three months, but I suspect that it will be for five, knowing our luck. It was a real chore packing and moving, but I hope the trip turns out to be worth it. All the lieutenants are living in a two-story building, and we have flush toilets and running water. Right now it's pretty disorganized, but I imagine things will be orderly by the time the month is out.

Our move, of course, means we will fly in NVN [North Vietnam], but there are a variety of missions, and we have had more training than anyone else, so we should have no problems. I really hope I can make it home in January, but I can't count on it.

The living conditions are nicer and the club is only a block away, so I am hoping these three months go real fast. If it is five, I hope they go even faster. My ear is all cleared up now, and I'm ready to fly. I have not flown once this month. Do not worry about me, my chances of coming home are as good as when I left, probably better.

Thank you for the great long letter, clippings, and picture, but where is the one of you? I am so glad you are impressed with your savings, and hope we can keep it when I get home. I sure hope we can stop worrying about Brad when I get home. I really think he is all right, but I tend to worry just the same. Love him too much, I guess!

I agree with Lemay [USAF General Curtis LeMay]. I am tired, tired, tired of the way the war is going. We are doing so little compared to what we could, and people are still dying. I hope something happens before the year is out. By the way, McNamara [Secretary of Defense Robert McNamara] is going to be here tomorrow, so you will see Danang on TV. I might buy a motorcycle here. Transportation is really a problem. A motorcycle is a problem, too, so I don't know what I will do. The flowers you mentioned are Vietnamese. They really grow over here, and are real pretty. I don't know what will happen to my tomatoes [at Phan Rang].

I do not know what to think about being sent up here either. If I get home in January, it will be worth it, but there are rumors spreading on us having to spend a whole year or more. Everyone in the squadron is here. There are not any women around. The town is off limits, and this place is almost under siege, so you have less to worry about than when I was in Phan Rang.

Tell your Mom that I really don't want to buy a new car and I like the Saab as a second car for you. I also know it is not a great cross-country machine. Remember Dakota? Also, tell her not to give you any ideas about becoming a bitch. You are fine the way you are. I really do not think anyone takes advantage of you. I love you because you are nice, and that is what really counts. What I want is a woman that acts like one. Those who act like men should be treated as such.

Well, I have a million things to do, so I will reluctantly close. I hope you know that your letters are the biggest morale factor I have here. They almost alone can create a good mood in me. Please write me and love me though I am so far away and gone so long I am nearly a stranger.

Love, Gary

Three days later, I got disappointing news about the length of my tour. My squadron seemed to get a tough break compared to others in the 366th.

15 October 66

Dear Wife and Son,

Well, as I feared the news has officially arrived. The combat tour is now one year or one hundred missions in NVN, so all my hopes of seeing you, my wonderful family, in early January are gone. I must now resign myself to another five months without you. This is really a hard blow to my morale. Every other 366th squadron that came over here is on its way back home. We will be the only one to serve both a year and a hundred missions, probably 280 or more missions here.

We also had our little three months in Alaska, so at the end of my year here, I will have been gone from my family all but 76 days out of the past year and a half. How can I even have a family when I am so little a husband and father? My boy will be two years and three months old. I will have seen him exactly one year of his life. He won't know me or I him when I get home. It is just too much to ask of you to live without a man and a husband, so now I guess I will really take a long, hard look at getting out of the service. I want to enjoy my family more than anything else. I cannot measure my duty to country against my love for you both—not in this stupid war. It is a real letdown for both of us, as I was counting on coming home in January, just a few months away. March seems like an eternity.

I will begin to work on Hawaii. I must see you before I completely lose all hope of ever having a normal married life. I am sorry to disappoint you also, you deserve a husband and Brad deserves his Dad.

Love, Gary

One spooky night I tried to place a call home via a Mars radio that patched calls into the U.S. phone system—our only method of talking to loved ones. I had received word that my R and R to Hawaii was scheduled for late November.

1 November 66

Hi Hon,

Well, I guess I won't praise you about writing any more. Every time I do, you mysteriously stop writing. I haven't received a letter from you for two days now. I expect your next letter to acknowledge the good news about Hawaii, so I'm really looking forward to it.

I spent about four hours last night trying to call you, to no avail. The Mars radio station was having difficulties, so no luck. Let me describe what I went through. Then you will know how much I love you. First, it was about 1030 at night, dark except for the flares burning overhead. It was raining and I was walking. The Mars station is about two miles away. And I was stumbling along in the mud holes, without a flashlight, carefully passing guard posts on the way. Thank God I do not look much like a Vietnamese! Finally, a truck comes along and I get a ride most of the way in the back of the truck—still raining. Then, as I am walking through the mud, completely off the road now, I find that behind the fence on my right is the guard dog compound (loud snarl).

Finally, I reach the station and find my name is number two on the list. A good deal at last. After waiting until 11 p.m., the radio operator informs us that he cannot start placing calls until midnight (10 a.m. your time). So we wait. Our waiting room has no chairs, just a board placed on some sandbags, but plenty of mosquitoes that are attracted by the light and my warm bod. Every time one bites me, I wish I had kept on taking my malarial pills—the ones that always give you the trots. But again, I figure malaria is the least I have to worry about.

Well, finally at 1 am, the radio operator announces all he can get is static, so we might as well go home. That is fine except now it is raining hard and no one can go home. The rain lets up and back I go through the mud. It is deeper now. I walk along waiting for another truck to come by, watching the flares overhead and listening to the artillery. Pretty soon

I begin to wonder where all the trucks are, but along I walk, wishing I had my .45 with me now because it is very dark and the VC are all around us every night making probes. Finally, along comes an Air Police truck. They stop and say, "Where are you going?" I say, "To the compound." They say, "This road takes you to town." I say, "How about that, I thought things were a little dark." They say, "That's OK, there's a guard post down the road. He would have stopped you." I say, "Where is the base?" They say, "We'll give you a ride." I say, "Thanks." So I go to the club and eat an omelet, and have several drinks.

It turned out that I was walking down a perimeter road, and snipers usually shoot at trucks once in awhile on that road. There I was walking along whistling, so no guard would think I was trying to infiltrate and shoot me. So, maybe I will try to call you again, but I don't think I will for a year or two. You can see, Hon, things are not very simple here at times, but you know I love you because I tried at least.

The twenty-fifth had better come pretty soon. If I keep having sexy dreams about it, I will be too worn out when the time comes.

Love, Gary

32. Night Missions

I preferred night missions over North Vietnam. You could see their guns firing, and they could not see you (unless you went below the flares). And you could spot the SAMS when they left the launcher. Most of our night missions were two-ship interdiction and armed reconnaissance.

The flight lead carried flares and CBUs. Number two carried rockets, or napalm. The lead took off and two followed after ten seconds and established a three-mile trail position on radar. The lead navigated to a choke point, or target, and called.

"Dropping the flares."

Then two started a shallow dive and was in position to fire when the flares went off. You had to be ready. The flare ignition caused trucks to careen off the road into the jungle like cockroaches scrambling when a light comes on in a house.

One night I got steep and pulled out below the flares, which illuminated me. The gunners gave me their best. I really thought I'd bought it as I jinked through the tracers all around me. Shells went right over my head. I remember thinking that I could reach up and touch them. I was *certain* I was going to see the actual bullet that would kill me. Amazingly, they all missed.

After landing I spent a lot of time with my flashlight inspecting my plane for bullet holes, finding none. I was astonished.

Your GIB was invaluable at night. He could keep you from getting too steep and fast. He also was handy when you got vertigo. I had a bad case of it one night. I was flying close formation through different cloud levels on the way to North Vietnam when the gyros in my head got so screwed up I actually believed my leader flew us through a complete roll. I kept asking my GIB which way was up. We finally broke on top of the clouds and I could see stars. My gyros reset and I was all right for the rest of the flight.

Dong Hoi was a river choke point just above the DMZ (demilitarized zone dividing North and South Vietnam). It was a key supply point for the enemy on the coast, and a good place for activity. The enemy had a lot of guns and was accurate, downing several aircraft. They once brought down five in two hours. We hated their gunners.

I was flying two, carrying napalm. As I circled low over the sea to come up the river, my lead was about to flare the river crossing. But before he could, the guns began to fire, which meant valuable targets were around. When I turned in from the sea, the guns were firing at my leader right on my nose. I was pissed, and I did a crazy thing. They were after my leader and I would make them pay.

I flew up the dark river using moonlight reflecting off the river and the radar altimeter, not really a useful low-level tool in the

F-4. The gun positions (57 mm and 23 mm) went wild. As their tracers spewed in numerous wild traverses, trying to find me, they looked like sparks from pinwheels. I went over some of them at two hundred feet and 480 knots. I could see them but they couldn't see me. I made four passes, taking out four gun positions that night. I was mad, flushed with adrenaline. We never dropped flares.

I was still excited during our debriefing, but later I slowed down and thought. I had a dragon inside me that came out in combat. It was a scary dragon. It fed on adrenaline. I needed to suppress it. I lost control when it came out.

It's unwise to make multiple passes on multiple gun positions. The odds aren't in your favor. If I wanted to go home, I needed to control the adrenaline that fed my dragon and use my head. My GIB, having seen all those tracers, thought the same, I'm sure.

Another night mission was just above the DMZ. This time we had a flight of four and a fast FAC flying an F-100. For good measure we also had an AC-130 Spectre gunship with three 20 mm Gatlings and three mini guns. The combined firepower from that one plane was eighteen thousand rounds per minute. The gunship had light panels on the top of its wings so we could spot it from above.

It was an aerial circus—an inverted cone of black airspace over the ground with six airplanes navigating it at over four hundred knots The gunship was below in a left-hand orbit, and the F-100 was above the AC-130 in a right-hand orbit. The four F-4s were diving down through those two orbits, the top lights of the gunship visible only when the C-130 was turned the right way. We couldn't see the FAC or each other at all.

Flares were dropped. A truck convoy was spotted and hit and secondary explosions went off. There was fire on the ground. Tracers came up, more went down. The night looked like a giant, upside-down fourth of July display.

One night I was on the schedule to fly number two with my flight commander, Major Vickery. It was a "sky spot" mission. We were to bomb from thirty thousand feet, guided by a ground radar site. We'd fly level, like big bombers, and the radar site would guide us to the target and call the release point for our bombs. It was a low-value mission designed to harass the enemy. We usually bombed some remote jungle position, probably only waking a few monkeys.

Incredibly, that night we carried only two 250-pound bombs each. The F-4 could carry twenty-three when fully loaded. It seemed the Air Force and the Navy were in a contest to outdo each other on the number of sorties flown, so we were going on a worthless mission, saving taxpayer money on bombs. I was in the front seat, so I wanted to go under any circumstances.

We climbed to altitude and contacted the radar site. I was on the wing in close formation, trying to keep a visual on my lead. We encountered heavy thunderstorms, the worst I'd ever flown through—intense rain, lightning everywhere, and turbulence ready to knock me off the wing position. It was like flying through a totally dark car wash, bumping over the brushes. Static electricity built up on both aircraft. The nose and leading edges of our planes glowed greenish-blue. It was surreal.

My eyes were locked on my leader as I desperately tried to control my aircraft and avoid a midair collision. Out of the corner of my eye I spotted a green-blue ball of fire roll up from in front of my gun sight, along the inside of the canopy over my head. It was like a gaseous lava lamp curling and changing shape as it spiraled aft. It was the static electricity called Saint Elmo's Fire.

I wondered where all that static electricity was going. Here I was sitting in a hollow aluminum tube outfitted with wings, filled with kerosene fuel, having two open flames (engines), and fitted with bombs. I hoped the engineers had all of this figured out, and that Saint Elmo was on our side.

The turbulence got rougher, if that was possible. The rain was so heavy I could hardly keep my lead plane in sight. I moved closer, my wingtip under, but overlapping my leader's wing. I felt the airflow from his wing through my flight controls. I had to stick on that wing like Velcro to avoid a fatal collision.

As we approached the drop point, the rain was so bad that the radar site lost us. We were vectored away, and the storm eased. I loosened my formation position.

The radar site asked Vickery if we wanted to make another pass. I thought *No! No! No!* But Vickery said, "OK."

Around we flew, back into the heart of the storm. Somehow I managed to hang on again. We dropped our bombs on cue. A few seconds later we saw four flashes far below as the bombs struck. The monkeys were now fully awake in the jungle.

We returned to Danang. I had had the formation ride and night thunderstorm penetration of my life. I wondered who'd been harassed the most—Coyote Flight or the enemy? I now hated sky spot missions, even from the front seat.

If you are in the military, you are an instrument of war. You can expect to be used and abused, but you don't want to have your life wasted. It's difficult to maintain a positive attitude when you are sent out to accomplish so little.

33. Twinkle, Twinkle, Silver Star

When we had to fly nights, the staff pukes, who only worked daylight hours, could be real troubling during the day.

My squadron had just finished our night missions, had a few drinks, and crashed under the mosquito nets to sleep. At about eight that morning our phone rang. Being closest, I was expected to answer. It was some officer from the command post. A senator was visiting from Missouri, and the brass wanted some officers from Missouri to meet him. I was pissed. “We have no one from Missouri in the squadron,” I growled and hung up. No sooner was I back in bed, it rang again. He said the same damn thing. This time I said, “All of our guys are from California or New York.” I hit the bunk again. It rang again, but this time a colonel was on the line. I was instructed to report to the command post *personally* with three other pilots in tan 1505 uniforms (which we never wore).

I woke the three guys I thought might not get too pissed and gave them the bad news. Wrinkled, we reported as ordered and were briefed that the senator would meet us and present us each with a medal. We were all to be from Missouri.

The senator arrived with a lot of brass. He was decked out in jungle fatigues.

"Where are you from, son?" he asked, shaking my hand.

"Kansas City," I said.

He told me I was a wonderful guy and that all of Missouri was proud of me. Then four citations were read about heroic combat exploits. Mine was so good that I got the Silver Star. The senator, beaming, was hustled off to the next event.

Wow! I got the Silver Star and didn't even know what mission it was for.

They made me give it back.

34. Marines on Fire

I was now leading flights. This was a big responsibility. The fate of seven other people depended on my judgment.

One night my flight of four pulled onto the taxiway in the quick check and arming area. Crew chiefs and bomb loading crews gave us a last-minute check and armed us with napalm. We used hand signals to communicate with the ground crews. Pilots had to show their hands outside of the cockpit so the bomb crews knew we wouldn't hit a switch or move a flight control and hurt them.

A Marine two-seat reconnaissance plane stopped on the taxiway right in front of us. I saw fire break out behind the cockpit and put my hand on the radio transmit button.

"Marine aircraft on the end of the Danang runway, you are on fire," I called. No result. I called again, this time with the tail number that I could just make out in the dark. "Marine aircraft, tail number 456, you are on fire."

The Marine pilots were seated side by side. I saw their white helmets turn towards each other. Then they looked over their shoulders and saw the fire. They jumped out of the plane, leaving it running right in front of mine.

Ground crewmen and bomb armers were under my airplanes, all four loaded with napalm, and a plane was on fire next to us. I goosed the left throttle up and down and the crewmen rolled out from under us.

I called the tower. "Coyote flight taking off." I gave the go hand signal and closed my canopy as we rolled down the runway. I was not waiting. I was going. My flight followed me as the tower radioed that we weren't cleared for takeoff.

Once airborne, my heart rate subsided. Now came the easy part. All we had to do was fly into North Vietnam and drop napalm at a low level in the dark.

The marine aircraft burned to the ground.

35. Coyote 22's Boo Boo

Bob Winegar and I met right out of pilot training. Both of us stood about six feet tall and weighed over two hundred pounds. I was slightly taller and better looking.

We were in the same group of combat aircrew in SERE (Survival, Evasion, Resistance, and Escape) school at Stead AFB in Reno, Nevada. The school was designed to train us to survive being shot down over enemy territory, evade the enemy at all costs, and deal with the realities of becoming a prisoner of war. It was very realistic: some of the instructors had been POWs, prisoners of war, in Korea.

The three-week course started with a week of classroom instruction covering woodcraft, escape and evasion techniques, code of conduct, and your responsibilities as an American fighting man—and even as a prisoner of the enemy.

The second week was POW training. At night our class of about 160 started out with a five-mile run to tire us out. We then were herded into a barbed-wire obstacle course. It featured machine gun fire, ditches, and guys walking around setting off explosions. We had to keep our heads down and crawl along, ultimately funneled into a "capture" point. Once captured we were treated roughly. A bag was placed over each head, which we couldn't remove, unless ordered to do so, without punishment. We were placed into four-by-four windowless cells with concrete floors and a single three-pound coffee can—either our toilet or food container. Our choice.

Inside the cell, bags over our heads, we listened for the guards moving down a crushed rock walk between the cells. When they abruptly opened the door, we had to be standing at attention wearing our bag or we were hosed down with a fire hose. Then two guards led each of us to a small box for "treatment." The box was the size of a small end table. I was jammed into it, legs folded under me and bagged head tucked down onto my chest. At my height and weight I was really wedged in. I fought to regulate my breathing and overcome the panic of claustrophobia.

After about twenty or thirty minutes (we had no watches) I was removed from the box, often unable to walk, having lost circulation in my legs, and led to an interrogation room with a one-way mirror. Behind it instructors graded our ability to deal with interrogation, which set us up psychologically to be happy to be with the interrogator. The grilling was meant to be tough. If caught in a lie (we were taught how to fabricate answers), we got "special treatment." One was water boarding (now politically incorrect)—head down on an inclined board, a cloth placed over the face, and water from a bucket poured up the nose. A man wouldn't drown but thought he was close to it. It made us understand that once we were prisoners, anything the enemy wanted to do he could. We developed a strong resolve to resist capture no matter how hurt, tired, cold, and hungry we became. Today I marvel at how politicized this procedure has become. It causes no lasting physical damage, only a strong incentive to make it stop and a greater willingness to talk to your captors.

We spent about three days in solitary, let out only for interrogation sessions or softening up in the box. A few of the class couldn't take the isolation and had to be removed from their cells

After this phase we were led to a barbed-wire compound. There we practiced group organization and communications. We organized to make escape attempts and learned how to resist as a disciplined military group with the senior officer in charge.

The third week we were bussed into the mountains at night and divided into groups of twelve or so to practice crew survival. Each of us was given six cereal bars, two potatoes, an onion, and half a pound of beef we made into jerky. We learned to hide in evasion shelters. Each morning the instructors tried to find us.

After three days of crew training we formed two-man escape and evasion teams, traveling at night and evading capture. As Bob Winegar and I were both large men, no one wanted to be a trek partner with either of us. We were supposed to carry our buddy to a road if he got hurt while we stumbled through the mountains at night, taking turns leading over the rocks and brush. So we ended up together by the process of natural selection. It was the beginning of a close life-long friendship.

For the escape and evasion expedition we were all brought

into a central camp and had our only hot meal of the week. We were briefed to expect an "attack" on the camp and were given coordinates to move to that night. As we finished the meal, cooked in big garbage cans, some brush on the hillside dropped and a machine gun opened up.

Bob and I had decided that our tactic would be to run as hard and as long as we could. We were both twenty-three and in good shape. We ran like hell, eventually going over the side of a ridge into a grove of thick pines and complete darkness. As we stopped to catch our breath, we heard something rustling along the ground, circling us. The hair stood up on the back of my neck. There were bears and mountain lions in the area. We each had a knife, plus one small folding shovel and a small axe, for defense. We each grabbed a tool and turned back-to-back, listening intently but not seeing anything that circled us. Simultaneously our courage failed us. Without a word we both broke and ran through the inky black. Today we still laugh at our response to what might have been only a rabbit.

After two nights of slipping and falling down mountains in the dark, evading "hostiles," at daybreak we found ourselves on the edge of a valley. Our final objective was across it. We could wait for night and make the trip around it, or cut across it and save a few miles. A ranch and road passed through it, making our capture probable if we were spotted. A stream ran along the road, and I convinced Bob that if we dropped down into it we could remain hidden and save ourselves a lot of time and effort.

The banks of the stream were steep, but low enough that I could keep my arms on top and hold myself out of the deepest cold water. Bob just wasn't tall enough, and he fell in several times. But the plan worked. We reached our final objective early, made a bed of pine needles, and slept all night under a poncho. We were so tired that the next morning we were surprised to wake up underneath four inches of snow.

Bob and I grew close on that trip and closer through the years. After Stead we went to F-4 training together in Tucson and were assigned to the 389th in Alamogordo. We served in Alaska, Vietnam, and Europe in the same squadrons. Our many adventures in many places in the world are the envy of our children. In some ways I'm closer to Bob than to my own two younger brothers.

I tell my Coyote 22 story to complete strangers, watching Bob grimace until he can tell his version. I start out saying that he was the only American pilot to bomb Danang while we still occupied it. (A Marine F-8 pilot did fire two five-inch Zuni rockets over the Doom Club one night as he left formation to land. We thought it was an enemy rocket attack and hit the deck. The Marine caught a lot of shit at the club afterwards.)

Bob was on a coveted front-seat night mission at Danang. During his take-off roll, an ejector rack fell off the aircraft. The rack and three bombs went skidding down the runway. Bob felt them go and felt his tire run over something. Fearing damage, he wisely kept the landing gear down and circled off to the sea. Flying slow, he had his wingman look him over. But the wingman's running lights didn't provide enough light to see clearly. Bob didn't know if he had lost a wheel or tire on one side. Over the sea he received clearance to jettison his bombs. They should have dropped in a safe mode. They armed, however, and surely woke up the Navy below.

Flying very heavy, low and slow, in bad weather, Bob dumped wing fuel. He tried to lose more weight by pulling his afterburner circuit breakers and dumping raw fuel out the back end of his engines. Bob is a smart guy, and the F-4 operating manual said the procedure would work. Somehow he got a hard light that torched the raw fuel and a big burst of twin flames shot out the tail of his aircraft. That was not supposed to happen. If the Navy below was not awake from the exploding bombs, they were now.

His aircraft still very heavy, he made an instrument approach. He dropped his tail hook and engaged the approach end barrier. Other than a blown tire, the plane was OK. The bombs skidding down the runway hadn't armed. But the runway was closed until the bombs were found and dealt with by ordnance disposal.

Bob had done an outstanding job flying that night: slow, heavy, night, weather—lots going on. But the next morning the daytime desk jockeys at the command post called and tried to blame him for the loose bombs. Those dummies who didn't fly the F-4 didn't know there was no possible way to set switches to drop a single bomb rack. It was some type of malfunction.

After I set Bob up with my Coyote 22 story introduction, I always sit back and watch him perform. He never lets his audience down. The stories I could tell about him would fill another book. His lovely wife, Barbra, who wasn't married to him when he was in the Air Force, found out a lot about him from me. Some of it's even true. If our Vietnam war stories get much better with time, we'll end up having won the war.

Now a retired radiologist living in Texas, Bob was an excellent fighter pilot. For five years we competed in everything we did in fighters. Now we compete on the golf course and in the field hunting. We'll go to our graves with one of us a golf stroke or a bird ahead of the other. He'll probably never forgive me for leading him down that cold stream in the Nevada mountains.

36. Rockets Ruin Your Sleep

Flying over North Vietnam was not the only way you could be a casualty at Danang. Almost every night we had a big fireworks display. The enemy perched in small boats in the river delta on the southern approach into Danang and shot .50 calibers at us during our final approach. When we made radio contact with the control tower, they gave us the runway in use, wind, altimeter setting, and location of Charlie, as our enemy gunner was called. There must have been more than one Charlie, because when he got too pesky we dropped bombs on him. The Marines laid out artillery and mortars after him, too. But like an energetic mosquito, he always came back.

Charlie never hit one of our fighters, although we saw his tracers from time to time on final approach. We were smart enough to fly blacked out. The unsuspecting transport pilots coming in from the States followed peacetime rules and flew with their navigation lights on. It was always humorous to meet a wide-eyed "trash hauler" at the bar after he took a couple of .50 caliber hits to his big bird. We always told him he should see the *big* stuff over North Vietnam.

Enemy mortars and rockets also came in. Of course the Marines returned fire. Along with the usual flares it was quite a pyrotechnic display. One enemy rocket hit the runway right behind one of our birds. The pilot aborted the take-off, had his bird checked out, then launched into North Vietnam. Another rocket hit one of our sister squadron's vans driving on a taxiway. The driver lost a leg.

One of our new guys got a Purple Heart for hitting his head running into the bunker in the dark during his first rocket attack. He didn't duck his head, hit the steel planking on top, and got a nasty cut . . . and a medal for being dumb.

This guy was a doofus. One night he was in Bob Winegar's backseat and closed the canopy on his hand. Trapped by the canopy, he couldn't reach his intercom mike button. Lucky for him Bob checked on him just before takeoff. Bob had to shut down the left engine and a crew chief crawled up on the wing and opened the canopy, freeing the errant GIB. Bob asked him to take off his glove and see if he was all right. When the GIB said, "It hurts," Bob had to abort the mission. He called the command post and reported his plane NORS (not operationally ready). They asked why. Bob replied, "GIB." The command post called him twice to figure out what that meant. We new aircraft commanders coveted our front seat rides, and Bob was pissed for a long time.

We veterans had a rocket drill. Most of the top bunks in our barracks were empty. So when we heard rockets coming, we reached up, pulled the top mattress onto the floor, rolled onto it, and pulled the mattress we were lying on over us, creating a mattress-pilot sandwich.

One night the bad guys got lucky. Their rocket hit the second floor of another squadron building across our street. When the attack subsided we got off our mattresses and went outside. There was a six-foot by eight-foot hole in the second-floor wall of their building. We thought there'd be casualties for sure.

Out of the building stumbled our buddies. They were in shorts and flip-flops, covered in white dust from the masonry, eyes big as saucers. But by good fortune the rocket had hit the crapper, and its walls had contained the shrapnel. No one had a scratch.

We all trooped down to the Doom Club in our shorts to celebrate our good fortune. We had to have a drink. It was impossible to sleep.

37. Special Forces Show

Many of us received an assignment to adopt a Special Forces camp. Our job was to visit the camp and draw up a plan for night defense—to create a method of getting in at night and in marginal weather and radio out procedures. Some of us got to visit our assigned camp to build the plan.

My visit started on a C-123 two-engine transport loaded with Vietnamese and crates of ducks and pigs. Boarding through the rear ramp of the C-123, I went forward to the cockpit and recognized the aircraft commander. A guy we called Chief, he'd been in pilot training one class ahead of mine. His claim to fame was getting lost on a solo cross-country flying into Mexico. He finally was guided back to base using a radio direction-finding steer. He was out of fuel and declared an emergency. All of the student pilots went out on the ramp to watch his "simulated flame-out approach." He did flame out, but landed safely. I checked his fuel gauges before the C-123 takeoff.

This pungent flight was followed by a chopper ride to the

Special Forces camp. The A team commander had arranged radio-out procedures. He had an arrow welded out of fifty-five gallon drums split lengthwise and mounted on a pivot. Other split drums were aligned adjacent to the arrow. The drums were filled with sand and diesel fuel. If radios were out, his plan was to light the arrow pointed in the direction he wanted us to deliver the weapons. Each of the other drums represented ten yards from the arrow as our aim point. Finally, he had an X built from the drums. When he lit the X, we were to drop everything but napalm on it.

Somebody pointed out that he only had covered bunkers for half of his cadre, and he replied, "When I light the arrow, only half of us will be left."

This was not a plan that fighter pilots were comfortable with.

Green Berets were weird people. I know, because my son Trevor is now one of them. I'm very proud of him. He's a warrior but is our strange child. Loves adrenaline.

Dick Johnson (who turned his bullet-riddled windshield into a coffee table) once found himself with extra fuel and close to his Special Forces camp. He got on the radio and called them. Alone, out in the boonies, Green Beret morale would be boosted by an Air Force flyby at low level. Dick formed up his flight in close fingertip formation for the air show with number two on his left, and three and four stacked lower on his right. Flying in close formation, the leader navigated and his wingmen watched only the plane next to them. A moment's distraction could cause a midair collision. The wingmen *had* to trust the leader not to run them into anything.

Johnson made a beautiful pass, except for one small item. He didn't allow room for his wingman to clear the camp's radio tower. Poor blue four flew smack between the tower and the guy wires, cutting off about four feet of each wing.

That afternoon I was manning mobile control, the small glassed-in trailer at the end of the runway. It was my job to check incoming flights for problems. Number four called in with battle damage. I put the binoculars on him on final approach as the fire trucks rolled. Four's gear was down. Everything looked OK, nothing hanging out of place. But something looked unusual, and I couldn't discern what it was.

He sped past on the runway. His wing tips were gone! The tower and guy wires had performed an almost perfectly symmetrical airframe modification, courtesy of the Green Berets.

The grunts at the Special Forces camp got their radios back up and gave us a call. They loved the flyby and wanted to know if our squadron could put an air show on for them again tomorrow.

I wonder what they did with those wing tips.

38. Short Round

The worst thing a fighter pilot can do is hit friendlies on the ground. We delivered napalm as close as ten meters to our troops at times, when the grunts were in deep trouble. This was scary for us, too. Napalm is a devastating weapon. One canister creates a fiery blast on the ground about thirty meters wide and 150 meters long, spreading flaming, sticky gel on everything. A miss could be lethal.

One day we had a close air support mission for some South Vietnamese troops. Two birds carried bombs and went in at a high angle. The other two carried CBUs and delivered them level at two hundred feet. CBUs were nearly as devastating as napalm. On each pass dozens of bomblets were released, each containing hundreds of ball bearings. Anyone or anything caught out in the open under a pattern of CBUs was destroyed.

For some reason the ARVN (the Army of the Republic of Vietnam, or South Vietnam) troops could not put out smoke to mark their position. They were positioned along a riverbed, in contact with the enemy, and marked their position with orange panels. We spotted the panels and the CBU birds were cleared to go in. The two birds with bombs orbited above.

At altitude a pilot has a certain terrain perspective and sense of speed. That orientation changes when the plane drops down low and flies fast. The illusion of speed certainly changes. Everything rushes at you, almost in a blur.

Our first guy picked up the wrong bend in the river as an aiming point and dropped a spread of CBUs right on the good guys. Distressed, the American advisor on the ground with the ARVN, and directing the air strike by radio, called us off.

My gut wrenched as I witnessed the smoke pattern of the CBUs exploding through the orange ground panels. "Oh, my God!" cried my GIB from the back seat. I will never forget that feeling. We left them with four casualties and sadness in our hearts. We hadn't just let them down, we'd killed them.

Bad news travels fast. By the time we landed, word of the incident had spread. While we were debriefing the mission, a freelance reporter poked his head in, obnoxious and aggressive. We were highly upset. I convinced him to leave with my .45. I still have an aversion to reporters.

We reported the incident. Nothing was covered up. We just badly needed some time alone to personally deal with the disaster.

39. R and R

Our military personnel were eligible for a week's vacation after six months in the theater. We could go to Japan, Thailand . . . just about anywhere but the States, except Hawaii. I chose that because I could afford to go there to see my wife and son. We had to pay for our dependents' expenses, but the military flew us for free.

I'd been trying to line up my R and R trip since August. Our transfer to Danang had delayed my break from the war in October, but finally I landed on the coveted list. My trip started about the twenty-second of November. Five days in paradise with my family! I was so anxious to see them. Brad would be two on December twelfth. I'd been deployed three months in Alaska, then eight months in Vietnam. I'd missed half his life.

Carole went to Hawaii a couple of weeks early and stayed in some cheap place. When our airliner landed, our dependents were bussed out to us. We boarded the bus and there they were—I saw my wife and son for the first time in nine months. Joy! I scooped up my son and put him on my lap, giving him a big hug. He wanted nothing to do with me and cried until he was secure on his mother's lap once more. I was a stranger to him. It took five days before he'd walk alone with me.

We wandered the beaches together and I was amazed that normal life was going on for civilians. The only war was on TV. Sometimes I picked out a place to eat and Carole told me, "We can't go in there." My son, a spoiled child who didn't like me sharing the attention of his permissive mother, was banned from several restaurants. Was this stranger really my kid?

The R and R disintegrated when the TV showed a number of planes shot down over Hanoi. Pictures of downed pilots also appeared in the papers. I had been lying to Carole about where our squadron flew our missions. Now she knew the truth and it hurt. It put a real damper on our family reunion. We made the best we could of our time remaining. Then I had to go back.

Our families accompanied us to a departure terminal. We then boarded a bus to ride out to the airliners taking us back to the war. We assembled to say our goodbyes (perhaps forever) and hug and cry. Carole was bawling. I tried hard to be a stoic warrior. After one last embrace, I turned to go to the bus. Suddenly Carole literally tossed Brad into the arms of a Red Cross worker. She grabbed me and, sobbing, would not release me. She had to be pried from me and escorted back to the terminal.

I sadly boarded the bus. As it pulled out I looked back, wondering if I would see my family again. There was Carole sobbing, running after that bus. To this day, the hardest thing I have ever had to do in my life was to get back on that plane. Going to war when we first deployed was the start of an adventure. Now I knew how dangerous and fickle war could be. There was no glamour in death.

To cope in war, you compartmentalized your life. You put friends, family, and the real world out of your mind as much as possible. I had to mentally gear up for combat once again.

Strangely enough, being shot at every day nearly became normal. I knew I could be killed. I also knew that my family left behind was subjected to the media coverage of the war every day. They wondered if the airplane announced as lost would be mine. My fears couldn't measure up to theirs. I knew what the real risks were. They only imagined them.

I returned to Danang and wrote this.

2 December 66

Dear Hon and Son,

Well, I made it back to Danang uneventfully, and I hope your trip home went as well as mine. Already I miss both of you, but I have good memories of my golden boy and golden girl to keep me warm. It is actually cold here, and right now I am freezing, but I bet it is colder in Omaha than it is right here. Boy, what a great trip. I really feel good that I got to see you both because Danang is dismal and just as moldy and dreary as when I left. The weather has been bad so no one has been flying very much, consequently no one expects to get forty missions by the tenth of January, and so it looks like I will be coming home sometime in February. About two months is all, and that is a short time compared to the previous eight.

You just about had me crying, too, when I got on that bus. I hope that will be the last sad tears you shed for me for a long time. I felt bad leaving you for the third time in a little over a year. Especially when I saw you cry on that ladies shoulder after the bus pulled out. Keep you chin up, hon. Things are going to get better.

Love, Gary

40. Downtown Hanoi

My flight drew a MIG cap assignment for our squadron's first mission to Hanoi. Our job was to screen the strike flights from enemy fighters. We were loaded with sparrow and sidewinder missiles. The target was the Phuc Yen airbase fuel storage area.

Our wing was going in naked. The F-105s had radar-jamming pods and SAM (surface-to-air missiles) warning gear to give them an edge over the SAM threat. Our wing leaders were anxious to get some MIG kills on our first trip "downtown" and hoped the F-105 countermeasures would protect us. A typical raid had sixteen flights of four carrying bombs (F-105s and F-4s) sequenced about every two minutes over the target. MIG cap flights, F-4 anti-SAM, F-105 wild weasels (SAM suppression), and other flights escorting jamming aircraft made up a strike package of about one hundred planes.

Our flight's task was to orbit the target area for *forty-three minutes* (I will never forget that number) and keep MIGs off our strike flights. They used the same route in and out of the target area flying at a lower altitude. The total mission flight time was about five and a half hours. We refueled from KC-135 tankers on the way in over Laos, and again on the way back. F-105 and F-4 wings from Thailand participated in the raid.

We were briefed on the MIG threat, gun positions, and SAM sites. The SAMS were Russian-built SA-2 missiles, which could reach fifty thousand feet. They were described as twenty-seven feet long, traveling about Mach 2 (1,500 miles per hour). We wondered what they'd look like.

At that point the North Vietnamese had about 130 SAM sites. We hadn't hit them because our leaders feared trouble if we killed their Russian advisors. This proved to be a bad decision for us. We paid in blood.

We were briefed that there were twenty-six active SAM sites near our orbit point. My flight was assigned to hit the tankers over Laos, flying at about thirty thousand feet towards Hanoi, just north of Thud Ridge, heading southeast, then orbiting the target area.

Major Drury Callahan was our flight leader. He was one of the few squadron members with air combat experience in Korea against MIGs. Dan Dugan was his backseater. Captain Ed Montgomery and Bob Wickman were crew number two. Our element lead, number three, had Captain Jim Thompson and Willy Rudd. Martin and I flew number four, tail-end Charlie.

Our flight of four flew in tactical formation, a combat spread, with about 1,000 to 1,500 feet of separation between planes so we could look for trouble. Because we flew number four, clearing our six position (rear) was our primary lookout. On top of a solid cloud bank, we maneuvered, rapidly weaving and pulling Gs, looking for trouble.

As we rolled out of a right turn I cranked my body around to check our rear. Two SAMs were coming up fast, real close. I shouted into the radio, "Break, break!" but my call was too late. I watched the direct hit on one of our wingmen on the left.

Martin pulled Gs like crazy as we broke into the second missile. All I could do was watch it come at us, nose hunting through the air. I hoped my neck wouldn't break from the G load. One of our flight disappeared into an orange fireball, blackened chunks flying off the aircraft. I couldn't tell if it was our flight lead or number two.

Two more missiles were coming, and we maneuvered for our lives. Martin and I were now alone. Our wild evasive action broke up our flight. We couldn't see anyone. We'd lost our mutual protection. We were playing defense now, just trying to survive. We made several radio calls, finally finding Thompson, our element leader. We rejoined him.

After an eternity the flight leader, Drury Callahan, called, "Two is hit. We are heading 240 [southwest]."

Our combat capability was cut in half. The adrenaline was bursting. We were targets, in range of lots of guns and SAMs. Low clouds covered the target area. Below us the strike flights maneuvered towards Phuc Yen, but the weather wasn't favorable.

Amid the chaos, a wild weasel bird went down near the target area. Emergency beepers went off. The radio chattered as flights commenced search and rescue. It was a real circus, with our remaining flight of two in the center ring. We orbited the assigned area to cover the strike flights as they approached the target. Every flight encountered low clouds near the target and, in turn, radioed that they were turning back. Eventually each bombing flight returned home.

Hanoi itself was cloudless. This meant the two of us high overhead were the main targets for all SAM sites in the area. And there were lots. Nine more SAMS fired at us, for a total of thirteen aimed at our flight. (I was born on May thirteenth and always thought of thirteen as my lucky number.) We could only spot them visually, then turn hard into them to outmaneuver so they missed. It was a ballet of death.

As we maneuvered we could tell which SAM was addressed at us. It guided on us and us alone. It was *very* personal. Flak, on the other hand, was nonspecific. I liked to think it was aimed at the other guy. When a SAM guided on me, the universe shrank to the airspace containing my plane and the missile searching for me. Nothing but staying alive mattered. My asshole also shrank. This was called puckering up.

Over the junction of the Red and Black Rivers outside Hanoi, the last of the thirteen SAMs fired at us that day, finally driving us from altitude. As we dove to evade, below us appeared a wide curtain of black flak explosions. The Hanoi area antiaircraft gunners were taking their turn. Down through the grey, menacing cloud of flak we went, reversing hard to miss the SAMs, then still under a lot of Gs, pulling hard back up through the flak again. The air around us was crowded with lethal steel projectiles.

"Let's get out of this valley," our element leader called. "They are trying to kill us."

No shit!

The entire mission ultimately failed. All the strike flights aborted the main target and headed home. Our MIG cap mission over, we could go back to base. We really needed to find our tankers because we were low on fuel, but we had two more hours to fly. The most dangerous part of our mission was over. Forty-three minutes of hell.

We cleared the Hanoi area fast. Our two aircraft had taken the brunt of the defenses that day but were unscathed. Welcome to Hanoi.

Exiting North Vietnam we tanked up over Laos, listening to radio calls for signs of our two lost wingmen. More than one plane had gone down, and confusion reigned. The search and rescue efforts failed and we left dead or captured comrades behind. When we landed at Danang, I needed help getting out of the cockpit. I was drained, still worried about our number two. We reached the command post for debriefing.

"Where are lead and two?" they asked. Who knows? Then the phone rang. Lead reported from Udorn, Thailand. He had escorted two there safely. Unbelievable! They were alive! I felt certain, seeing their plane disappear in the fireball and parts falling off, that they were surely dead. Fate was fickle once again.

Both Ed Montgomery and Bob Wickman are well today. Ed sent me this account of his actions that he had shared with Bob about that day.

So into route pack six we went, in fluid four as we had no jamming pods. Our visual lookout was to protect the six o'clock of the other element and vice-versa. I was told by Will Rudd later that he actually saw a glow come out of the under cast, thought it was triple-A tracer, and reported that to Thompson—and by the time they both saw the "glow" make a corrective turn into us, it was too late to say anything. But that was how they were able to tell Callahan that we'd been hit. They saw it happen!

As you remember, our first clue that anything was wrong is when we felt the *whump* and the fireball rolled around the canopy, and we were knocked into a steep dive. Your info on the reconstruction of where the missile went off was news to me, but sounded absolutely accurate: just below and behind us. The reason for the dive was the nose trim had failed full nose down . . . but the dive probably saved our lives because it blew out the fire and caused the second SAM, the one that you saw, to miss us.

A side note: Flying the airplane back with full nose down trim and all three stab augs inoperative (stability augmentation system) was interesting. My right arm hurt for two days afterwards, but at the time I didn't mind at all!

You're right that Drury, as lead, was calm. As we were plummeting down he called and asked, "Two, are you going to be able to get that under control?" To which I replied something like, "I'm doing my best." As I recall (and I wrote in my report) we finally pulled out at about 16,000 feet and not far above the undercast just west of Hanoi. Initially we headed up Thud Ridge, just to get some non-populated terrain under us in case we still had to eject. Drury was, in fact, actually able to catch us and he gave us a very close one side to the other look—and then he and Dan moved off, way over to one side of us. I asked him if anything was wrong and he answered a bit apologetically that we were losing fuel so badly that he wanted a little distance between us in case we blew up. I recall we made the decision to stay in the airplane, without any urging from lead.

We not only had a centerline tank, we had both wing tanks for extra fuel. The centerline had blown completely off, as you relate (as the underside rear of our aircraft suffered a hell of a lot of damage). As we exited the area and turned to the southwest in order to try and get to some safe countryside (going northwest up Thud Ridge was not the way we wanted to continue) I tried to get the wing drop tanks to feed, but they were force fed by air off the engine compressor section and apparently had so many shell holes in them that they couldn't feed. So I jettisoned them to lessen our drag and let us get a little closer to something safe. The "good" news about all that was that their taking all that damage may have been what protected our main gear so that both main tires still had air when we blew them down.

As I recall, Drury simply told Thompson to take the other element home while he stayed with us; I don't remember them chasing any MIGs. I do remember, though, that they told us that two more SAMs were fired at us as we left the area, but we were obviously over nineteen miles away by that time. (Maybe those were the streaks you saw.) In thinking about the whole mission afterwards, I reasoned that the SAM site we didn't know about shot two missiles successfully at that F-4 strike flight, fired two missiles at us pretty much successfully, and then fired their last two missiles at us in vain. At least we ran them out of missiles!

One other thing. The conversation you remember about our airspeed decreasing happened because the pitot tube was also in the tail that took such damage and the airspeed eventually decreased all the way to zero. That's why Drury flew close to us when it came time to lower the gear (and also we weren't losing fuel at a great rate by then!) to make sure we were under the gear-lowering speed. Then, on final approach, we were able to use the angle of attack indication to make sure our approach speed was OK. Thank the Navy for the fact that we had an angle of attack indicator and a tail hook!

Ed landed at Udorn, successfully making a barrier engagement. Their plane was completely out of fuel. Those at Udorn said it was the worst shot-up F-4 ever to make it back from North Vietnam.

Montgomery and Wickman arrived from Thailand the next day. They related their wild, scary story. They had the "deer in the headlights" look about them because the C-47 sent from Danang to pick them up almost crashed on takeoff from Udorn.

Since we didn't hurt the target, it remained on the schedule. The North Vietnamese knew we'd be back. We knew that they knew. They'd be even more ready for us.

We briefed this same target, then had a weather hold, and then a cancel. This was the worst possible psychological scenario, briefing about the heavy defenses, reviewing our losses on that target, gearing up, and then waiting for clouds to clear. Tension. Tension. Some guys vomited after each briefing.

Finally, the last briefing over, our squadron got the "go."

Montgomery and Wickman were assigned to this mission as a spare—they would start engines and fill in if one of the strike birds aborted.

Our flight gear was in a Quonset hut across from our squadron building. As we geared up for combat, Wickman rose up as he donned his G suit and hit his head on a steel overhead rack, fell, and banged his head on the floor. He was out like a light.

Montgomery needed a replacement. GIBs grabbed Wickman's maps and raced back to the squadron building. Mick Larkan had the duty flight, so he felt safe. But his luck was about to change. Rushing into the squadron building, the crews found Mick standing behind a counter with a scheduling board behind him.

"Mick, Wickman has dead bugged. You need to take his place."

Larkan didn't have his game face on. "I'm not briefed." (Too bad!) "I don't have any maps!" He was handed Wickman's. No more excuses. Poor Mick, gone from safety to danger in thirty seconds. Fortunately the spare wasn't needed and Montgomery and Larkan didn't fly. Mick's luck had returned.

Two of our squadron mates didn't return from that mission. Wickman recovered, got cleared to fly again, and retired a full colonel, as did Montgomery.

I thank Ed for his account of the mission. We started out in the same formation but had very different flights that day.

41. Burns and Ducat

On December 2, 1966, our wing returned to Phuc Yen to finish the job. We were going over heavily defended targets as well as into low overcast conditions, both dangerous. When a SAM launched it had a big plume of flame and blew up a lot of dust, easily spotted leaving the launch site. Once it accelerated it had a smaller sustainer rocket, making it harder to detect. When the SAMs popped out of the cloud deck going over 1,500 miles per hour, we had little time to see them and react.

Burns and Ducat flew number three inbound to Phuc Yen. Their flight lead lost his inertial navigation system and asked them to take the lead and navigate the flight to the target. Moments after, a SAM hit them. Their wingman saw two good chutes, but they landed where they'd probably be captured immediately. Burns was a POW at the Hanoi Hilton for over six years. Bruce Ducat didn't come back.

Many years later Burns told squadron mates he thought Bruce was shot during capture. We had all talked about what we would do facing the enemy after being shot down. Bruce said he would not be captured. No one knows to this day what happened.

Bob Winegar sent me his version of that mission.

THE MISSION: December 3, 1966

We briefed early for what was to be a very long day. Practically everybody in the wing was going. I think the target was known as JCS 5119, but whatever; it was in Route Pack VI, the Hanoi/Haiphong area. Some guys went there all the time, and my hat is off to them. We had spent our first seven months or so staying mostly in South Vietnam. Then in September we rejoined two other squadrons from Holloman AFB in what had been and would again be the 366th Tactical Fighter Wing. One of the squadrons stayed at Cam Rahn Bay. The other three were now at Danang, and flying routinely into North Vietnam, a much more dangerous place. Somehow I think air-to-air combat over Dallas would feel a little safer than over Hanoi, but of course I'm glad that's never happened. I remember not wasting a lot of time worrying about being dead. I was young and tough, or at least I guess I thought so, only not really, like Marine-tough or ROK-tough (Koreans), but tough enough with my two jet engines with big afterburners in my personal fighting machine that could go over 1,600 miles an hour-tough. It really seldom scared me that I might die. But I was very much afraid of being a prisoner. That would be hard duty. So after seven months of what was relatively safe I was not particularly thrilled to be getting my "opportunity in the big arena."

The largest briefing room was full of people and I swear some of them I'd been around for three months and hardly seen them before. We sort of knew all the guys from the Doom Club but really knew our squadron of maybe 50 guys best. So among all these friends and stranger-friends I'm writing notes and studying my maps while they brief us on the mission. About half, maybe two-thirds of the birds were in the strike force, and the rest of us flying MIG Cap. We would be staying up about 20,000 feet looking for MIGs to kill, only the MIGs weren't going to be there because the weather was crappy. So for the better part of an hour we flew around in tight turns, pulling no less than four Gs for all but a few seconds of course, reversals trying to make it impossible for ground-based radar to track us and kill us with a SAM. During the briefing I wrote down everything I could for the first 20 minutes, then realized there were so goddamn many AAA sites you couldn't have kept track of them all with a computer, which of course we hadn't yet even dreamed of. And since there would be an overcast layer under us and we couldn't even see the ground, there was a good chance we wouldn't even know where the hell we were for much of the flight.

Considering the weather our commanders could justifiably have scrapped the mission since the MIG protection would at no time be able to see the strike birds we were there to protect. It's worthy of note here that as the war progressed, some of our equipment was modernized a little. For example, they were now supplying our fighter planes with an electronic counter measures pod (ECM Pod). These were capable of warning the flyers if they were being painted by radar, and if they were being tracked by that radar, and ultimately if a SAM was launched at that aircraft. Since the F-4 units flying out of Thailand got the ECM pods first, and we were the only ones that still didn't have them, the command in Saigon had decided for a brief period we would discontinue our flights into Route Packs V and VI until we also had this extra defensive device. This seemed a very reasonable decision to most of us. However one or two of our beloved leaders personally went to Saigon to beg for our return to "the big arena" without the pods. They were being denied some glory, I guess. As a lieutenant I was not privy to the decision process, but this was the story we got at the time. The same people who got us back on these missions without ECM protection would now send us to Hanoi above the clouds. From above the clouds you can't even see a missile launched from the ground, and have no clue it's coming until it screams up at about Mach 3 (three times the speed of sound), usually exploding in a big ball of fire and debris—luckily in my case not close enough to kill us. By the way, Thailand is a nicer place than Danang, but with overall a tougher mission, since they went more frequently way up north and we still did some work in slightly less defended areas of North and South Vietnam.

On most of our previous missions we took two to four airplanes, usually from the same flight, a sub-unit of a squadron, with ten or twelve pilots typically. We briefed in a small room, around a table with eight or fewer guys who all knew each other very well personally and as pilots. We knew the strengths and weaknesses of all of them pretty well (mostly strengths, of course, but not entirely tongue in cheek since we were all by then very experienced and I daresay excellent pilots).

This briefing was like no other I had ever seen: more information from the intelligence staff, and more complex overall, more briefers talking about more little details. There would be rendezvous with tanker aircraft both going in and coming out, and tactical briefings for both the bombers and the air superiority aircraft. The length of the briefing and the overall tenor were more than usually intense. Although we were always pretty serious when we briefed, our closeness and familiarity with same-flight personnel and our usual missions allowed for some levity. Not this time. I remember distinctly feeling unusually serious about the impending mission but was not yet truly afraid, although it felt a little like we were about to drink the Kool-Aid (intentionally anachronistic).

Well, after a very long time the briefing ended and most of us went to the head for a last piss, or out for a cigarette. If you joined the service in those days and didn't smoke they would be glad to teach you. Most of those poor old bastards never could quit. I went for both actually, but felt a little left out since four or five guys at a time would be in the head puking their guts out. I realized then they had been on similar missions before and the apprehension and solemnity I felt were rising. We would be in the air for about five hours, counting tanker time, and that last piss just might keep your flight suit dry until you got back. So we made it the last stop before going to the personal equipment shop to pick up helmets, masks, and harness with its radios, handguns, water bottles, flares, and other personal evasion/survival gear. These were well maintained and even kept clean in this sometimes-nasty environment by a very dedicated enlisted crew whose only job it was to take good care of our stuff. They were great guys and I thank them here again now. We carried no parachutes. They stayed in this aircraft. We attached them to our harnesses as we prepared to start engines.

On this particular trip to get my PE (personal equipment) off the rack I had a slightly unusual experience. It was actually necessary for me to straddle the left leg of one of my comrades who was scheduled to fly this mission, but had hit his head on an overhead equipment rack and "deadbugged" right there on the floor, and clearly not going with us. Let me add that a day or two before he had been on a similar mission and took a direct hit by a SAM over north Vietnam, ultimately totaling the aircraft, but with just enough hydraulic pressure left to limp out of the target area, full of holes with major damage but still barely flying. His front seater was Ed Montgomery, a very fine pilot and the only man I ever knew well who had graduated from the Air Force Academy in the class of '59, the first graduates, only 207 of them. (I knew mostly guys from '60 through '66 since we were there at the same time.) I have no doubt that Ed's airmanship and skill saved their lives, or at least saved them from ejecting that day. He was also a very fine officer. Anyway, they made it over one river, then another, and eventually limped into Thailand where they plopped it on the runway and escaped the wreckage with their lives, and not much else. They bulldozed that bird off the runway and scavenged a few parts. Two crew chiefs took turns tossing a football through the hole in the mostly absent tail, or vertical stabilizer, as it is properly known. It sits high off the ground and the hole was huge, several feet in diameter.

Ed completed his tour and left from Saigon in late January '67 together with the rest of us who had gone over as a squadron, the 389th Tactical Fighter Squadron, and survived. The backseater I never saw again, after calling someone to help him off the floor and out of the PE shop and getting my gear.

We rode in little vans to the aircraft, pre-flighted them in the usual manner. We carried only missiles and a 20 mm cannon pod hung on the centerline, with external wing tanks for extra fuel. Some of the missiles would kill at over ten miles, but of course we were not allowed to shoot at anything not visually identified so the heat-seeker missiles and the cannon were the weapons of choice. Following pre-flight we got in, strapped in with a little help from our crew chiefs, and started engines, taxied out, took off in two ship formation, rejoined as four ships, and flew in loose formation toward the target. We filled up with fuel from airborne tankers going in and coming out as planned. Pretty routine for a fighter pilot.

Our only job that day was supposed to be killing MIGs. Turned out our only job was to keep from being killed by SAMs we could neither detect electronically nor see launch. Usually our first clue was another goddamned explosion nearby. Of course, we did our mission, looked all over for enemy aircraft, listening carefully to the incessant chatter of the strike birds for any clues as to where they might be getting harassed by pesky little enemy aircraft, but the enemy never came up. They never did when the sky was so full of SAMs. They might get hurt. With no visual aids, and of course no

VOR [Very High Frequency Omni directional Radio range], Tacan [Tactical Air Navigation], or other navigation aids like we have at home, we had some difficulty staying in a two ship and staying in the area over the strike.

We got some help from Elint [U.S. Navy's Electronic Signals Intelligence] aircraft. These guys were orbiting out over the South China Sea in big birds with lots of electronics so they could really see the whole clusterfuck going on over the target, and they helped somewhat. In the back seat that day, behind a different Gary, my usual front seater, I was also spending time scanning the radar for any clues of enemy aircraft with my four G, over-one-hundred-pound head leaned over in the scope. I grunted at one point after one particularly high G maneuver when my face bounced off the radarscope and Gary said, "What's the matter?" I answered, "You're killing me." I suppose he might have thought I was hit and relaxed the Gs ever so slightly, probably reflexively out of concern for me, but only for an instant as I immediately added, "pull harder." Remember we had been almost an hour at around four Gs. It was not unusual to do a bit of grunting with the straining (so called M-1 maneuver) of keeping the blood out of your legs and gut, assisted with an inflating G suit, which pushes back harder the more Gs you pull, but with a little personal effort was occasionally helpful. We went in as a four ship, I think. Got separated into two two-ships. I think Bob Rossmeisel and Rollie Truitt were in the other bird. The four of us were frequently together. I remember thinking Rollie's goddamned phi beta kappa key wasn't worth a shit about then.

We couldn't see the strike force, which went in under the clouds, and if they'd been bounced by a MIG we couldn't have helped much anyway, so just what in the hell were we there for? I felt like a skeet target would feel, except that we had to orbit the great Hanoi skeet range in the sky for about an hour while the little bastards fired SAMs up through the clouds at us. I lost count of the explosions I witnessed, but saw several of them hit airplanes, with metal raining out of the sky all over the place. For the only time in my life I now knew terror. Not much scares me after this experience. I don't have the historical record but recall later being told we (America) lost seven fighter aircraft on this mission. And only some of these were up high with us. Most were probably in the strike force bombing some silly-ass bridge for the hundredth time with our WWII bombs and, even dumber, more predictable tactics straight out of the Johnson/McNamara basement of the White House. This was the year in which I lost faith in leadership as practiced by most incompetent people, and in government. It's also when I decided to think again about medical school, rather than this admittedly usually lots of fun career. I still have no idea if the strike was of any value to the war effort.

Finally the strike was over and it was time to leave the area, still in a series of tight turning maneuvers until we were well out of SAM range. The sky was now full of airplanes and we were trying to rejoin the flight we came in with and get back to the tankers. It would really piss you off to run out of kerosene at this point. We were just beginning to relax when we heard, among the other chatter, "Chicago Three is down in the target area." I was exhausted and had no idea who that was. At this point I was stricken with grief for my comrade now in grave danger. Almost simultaneously came the relief that "it ain't me." Don't try to second-guess that one either, sports fans, unless you've been there, in which case you already know it.

Gary kept a more complete list of who was up there that day and said "Chicago Three, that's Don Burns." "Also Bruce Ducat," I added, always conscious of the back seat since I spent a lot of time there. Most backseaters were guys my age and most of them really good friends. Sadly, Chicago Three was Don Burns, my flight commander, and his usual back seater (and frequently mine, when I was in front). We made it home without further incident and probably drank even more than usual.

When I first met Ducat I told him "Winegar rhymes with vinegar." I looked at his nametag and he said "Ducat." I said, "Rhymes with fuckit." He loved it. Just then Mike Syptak (an aggie) walked up and said, "What are you going to rhyme with Syptak?" I said after a moment's reflection, "Nuthin', I'll just remember cat piss spelled backwards." We all enjoyed this kind of give and take. It's part of the closeness comrades in arms develop and appreciate together, but seldom with outsiders. Last conversation I had with Bruce I remember him telling me about his trip to Thailand. And I remember he said if he ever had a son he thought he'd name him Donald. Good sense of humor, that guy. We also discussed our fears, really the biggest one being taken prisoner. I think we just denied thoughts of death even though it was all around. The biggest fear of being a prisoner was that you would not be tough enough. The treatment was known to be horrible. How would you be able to be one of the ones who told them all to kiss your ass when they were torturing and maiming you? Some guys were that tough. We really didn't want to know if we weren't. I may never have disclosed this before but Bruce told me he would never be a prisoner. I saw Don Burns again in August of 1973. All that time he'd been a prisoner of barbarians, while I enjoyed a great tour in Germany and all over Europe and North Africa, and had the opportunity to complete medical school and father my first child. Yes, you feel guilt at the disparate fortunes.

I was by then an intern at an Army hospital in Tacoma, WA. It was virtually next door to McChord AFB. I made a few calls and bummed a ride on an Air Force plane with some other Rats to the first real reunion of the Red River Valley Fighter Pilots' Association, also known as the River Rats (Hanoi, not the Oklahoma border). My new Air Force buddies had a few laughs over my ugly green uniform with its Air Force Pilot's wings and a few ribbons we all got from the war. The POWs were released that spring, and all former reunions had been practice ones. Can't have a real one without the POWs. Don told me he was surrounded when he hit the ground and had no reasonable choice but to surrender. He said his captors indicated what he thought meant that they were going to take him over there, and he pointed, and shoot him. Later, since he never saw Bruce again, he realized that they were saying your buddy came down over there and they had killed him. Knowing Bruce's aversion to capture I feel certain he drew his pistol and was killed in the return fire."

Bob does a great job of relating the chaos we encountered on missions over Hanoi. We have deep respect for those who survived one hundred missions over North Vietnam, and even deeper reverence for our comrades who endured much worse as prisoners of the North Vietnamese.

This was our squadron's fifth aircraft loss. Our squadron's cost so far: two pilots killed and one a prisoner. It took me a few days to find the courage to write home. I fibbed a little and told Carole that I was flying over safer places than Hanoi. The mission date of our loss of Burns and Ducat was December 2, 1967. Bob remembers it as December 3 and I refer to the date as December 1 in my letter. The dates fade after forty years, but the mission memories do not.

11 December 66

Dear Wife and little son,

Finally, received another short note from you today, and now I am ready to write you something substantial. I hope you have not forgotten to get your passport photos taken, etc. Frostic received a letter from his sponsor, and it basically said that housing is scarce in Germany. Sending a limited power of attorney would help, as good places must be leased as they become available and there are not that many good places that compare to our standards. I should hear from my sponsor by the end of this week, and I will try to forward all the information to you as I get it.

I have only fifteen missions to go, and I am starting to get "get home fever" and anxious to see Germany.

Now, I guess I will tell you some bad news so you won't hear about it from someone else. Major Burns and Bruce Ducat were shot down by a SAM near Hanoi on the first of December. I did not really want to worry you with this news, but I figured you might find out from someone else, or accidentally hear from Bobbie Ducat some way.

Chritzberg was flying behind them on the wing and saw two good chutes, so they are most likely alive. Probably captured by now. There is no chance of rescue going in where they went down. If they can evade for a couple of weeks, they possibly could still be picked up, but since we heard no beepers, they probably were captured immediately.

I don't want you to worry about me too much because I am staying further south right now and my most dangerous missions are over, I hope. It was bound to happen, and we all expected it, but it is still tough. That was the mission Wickman passed out on in personal equipment. He is now in Japan in a hospital for tests.

The weather has been good here the past three days, so we are getting our "counters." You just don't worry too much. If I do get hit now, it is just fate because we have seen every phase of this war and know how to protect ourselves. I hear that Bobbie Ducat is taking the news pretty good, which is good. I am happy to be through flying in NVN by ten January. I will be on night schedule the twenty-first of this month again, so there is even less chance of my being shot down. I know you will worry, but you should be used to the thought by now, so try and have a happy Christmas. I may not be home by then, but ours will be happier than others we know.

I read the article on growth, and I am almost convinced that all Brad needs is his Dad around full time, and on a regular schedule. He is brighter than most his age, so maybe he is psychologically upset over his lack of a father. We will know as soon as I am home long enough. I know he will be OK when we are together again.

Talking about Christmas, I have enjoyed my presents already (you and Brad in Hawaii), so it has been a successful one. I will be home in person to give you your Valentine, though.

Other items of note, I have been submitted for a second and third DFC [Distinguished Flying Cross], and there are only thirteen more bombing days until Christmas. Tell me what your thoughts are on what we should sell or keep before Europe.

Love from Dad, over for Brad (drawing of Dad writing Mom in his BOQ [Bachelor Officers' Quarters])

42. Eyes and Balls Alone Won't Work

By early December 1966 our wing was flying deep into the Hanoi area. We didn't know it at the time, but ours was the only wing going in naked. The F-105 wings and F-4 wings based in Thailand had jamming pods and SAM detection gear. We had nothing but 20/20 eyeballs. But our leadership was anxious to get us into that fight so we could bag some MIGs. We were the ones who got bagged. Eight or more of our aircraft were lost or damaged by SAMs that first week over Hanoi. Poor tactics and lack of electronic countermeasure equipment had us facing a short life expectancy.

Flying in over broken overcasts, each flight of four depended on eight sets of pilot's eyes to spot the SAMs. We had no other means to detect them. If we spotted them in time we maneuvered to avoid them. It was a violent process. If we spotted a SAM coming up at us, we broke down into it hard, hard. This gave the SAM's guidance computer a maximum look angle change. The SAM then began to nose over, coming after us. As soon as it nosed over towards horizontal we rapidly reversed, pulling the nose up at a steep angle with lots of Gs.

The SAMS were faster and had small wings. We were slower with bigger wings, so we could turn inside the SAMs, making them miss. Some were still close. I am here today because a SAM's influence fuse failed to go off as one passed right in front of my nose. Several planes came back with the wing tips pulled off from the extreme G loads.

Due to our heavy losses, the higher-ups somewhere grounded our wing. We were not effective. (We were just fighting for our lives!) On a memorable Sunday morning (perhaps it was December 4, 1966), we were discussing what more we could do to stay alive. I will always remember one grim comment: "If this keeps up, we will all be dead by the end of the week."

Our wing sat down until radar-jamming pods could be brought in. They were bolted onto pylons, wires duct-taped along the wing. I can vouch for duct tape's ability to go one thousand miles an hour. The jamming pods worked as long as the flight stayed close. If somebody got thrown out of formation he stuck out like a sore thumb on enemy radar and got a Sam up his butt. Believe me, we saw some real fine formation flying once we got the pods.

We later got small scopes that let us monitor the radar threats. This gave us a heads-up to both SAM and MIG radar activity. We learned that if we were ready, and spotted them in time, we could make the SAMs miss. Our fear of them became manageable. Almost all of us would live, but I will always remember that first week over Hanoi, and that Sunday.

I will never forgive our political leaders for allowing the enemy to build over 130 SAM sites with impunity. And the terrible price we paid for that decision.

43. Doom Club

When you experience dire threats to your life on a daily basis, you become casual about your activities on the ground. No noncombatant can impress you. When you are in intense combat, you need to let off steam, and recharge your psychological batteries so you can face danger once more. For fighter pilots in those days, that meant drinking at the bar.

Our field mess was also the officers club, known as the Danang Officers' Open Mess, or as we called it, the Doom Club. Since we flew twenty-four hours a day, the bar was open all day. We played a lot of pranks and in general raised hell, when we were not scheduled to fly.

"Doom Club" was posted on a sign in front of the club. We loved the irony. Our superiors thought it was bad for morale. But we loved that name and would defend it against all political correctness.

We had a few casualties there. One of the games we played was "stop the fan with your head." The club had overhead fans with metal blades. The trick in stopping one was to climb up on a chair, covertly place your head on the hub, slow the motor down, *then* whip your head out in between the end of the blades. We challenged all transport crews (trash haulers, in fighter-pilot talk), civilians, and other noncombatants to be as tough as fighter pilots and stop the fan with their head.

Our trick was to distract the trash haulers while one of our guys got his head out on the end of a fan blade. We then would place a chair strategically out near the end of another fan and challenge the victim to step up and be a man, and stop the fan. The usual result was several bloody gashes in the victim's head (head wounds bleed a lot) as he vainly tried to stop the metal blades. If we were in a generous mood, we would call an ambulance ahead of time.

All of the aircrews that stayed overnight in a combat area got combat pay. Ours was $65 per month. We earned ours, so felt we should make the overnighters earn theirs, too.

We also did parachute landing falls off the bar and there were endless games of "dead bug." This was played in fighter clubs around the globe. A pilot was "it" if he lost the prior game. He had the ability at any time he was in the bar to yell "dead bug." Every man in the bar had to fall to the floor flat on his back and wiggle his arms and legs up in the air like a dead bug. The last guy judged to have hit the floor bought the bar a round of drinks. So you saw guys push barstools over backwards as everyone crashed to the floor. The last guy down was "it" until the next round. You always tried to keep your eye out for "it guy."

One thing we did not allow was other pilots to drink at our bar if they wore knife pockets on their flight suits. Fighter pilots wore

G-suits (which contain air bladders that inflate to compress legs and abdomen to prevent blackout under high G conditions) over their flight suits. Trash haulers did not. There was a parachute knife in a pocket on our G-suits. The flight suit pocket was removed. We didn't wear squadron insignia, so the way to tell who was who in the pilot hierarchy was to look for the pocket on the flight suit. No knife pocket meant a fighter pilot.

We had a big string of pockets we had removed hanging over the bar. Trophies of trash haulers vanquished at the bar. The procedure was to surprise the other pilot, two or more guys taking him over backwards, then one or two popping the stitches loose and tearing the pocket away. We then allowed that pilot to drink in our bar—preferably after buying us a round of drinks.

One night we came through the mess on the way to the bar and couldn't help noticing a white tablecloth and real china on a single table. It seemed our wing commander was entertaining a two star general, wearing a new flight suit. We discussed our rules of engagement and decided that if the general came into the bar, he must follow the rules.

This had to be a surgical strike. We had to let the general down, but not get him wet on the floor (after all, he was a general). This would take five of us: four to hold him horizontal off the ground and one to pop the pocket.

After dinner, in came our wing CO with the general. Our commander said, "Men, I would like you to meet—." Down went the general, off came the knife pocket, up went the general. We had pulled off a perfect strike.

Our commander was stunned. We all stood at attention. The general sputtered, "What is this about?" When we told him our rule he said, "Shit hot! I flew P-47s in WW II. Does that count?" Then he bought us a round of drinks.

Our commander joined us, looking a little flushed.

In the center of the bar, we had a big brass gong we rang whenever drinks were on the house. Critzberg once fired a spear gun down the length of the bar right through the gong. The spear embedded in a wall and fortunately didn't ricochet and kill someone. If you were shot down and recovered, the first place you went, if able, was not to the hospital but to the Doom Club to ring the gong. You had just cheated death and medical care could wait until you celebrated. Your comrades in arms joined the recovered crew in a boisterous celebration. More than one pilot appeared there with a broken arm, hobbling on a bad leg, wet from the sea, or with a compression fracture of vertebrae from ejection. The hospital could wait. We had to celebrate life.

One night a civilian contract worker showed up in our bar, drunk. He wanted to buy the fighter pilots a drink. We told him he had to ring the gong. Somewhere along the line we had lost the soft-covered gong ringer, so we used a regular claw hammer. The gong was mounted perpendicular to the bar.

Duff Green, from another squadron, was sitting at the bar with his back to the gong, conversing with the guy next to him. The civilian grabbed the hammer, took a mighty drunken swing, and hit Duff in the back of the head. Duff was out like a light. He was still unconscious when the ambulance arrived. We consoled the contrite civilian, and allowed him to buy several rounds.

The next morning we went to the hospital to see Duff, sitting up in bed with a big bandage on his head. "What happened?"

"Duff, you got hammered at the bar last night."

You can never trust civilians.

44. Accident on the Ramp

After one mission we stopped in front of the refueling pits. Other F-4s were there, plus a small crowd and an ambulance just pulling away. I climbed down the boarding ladder and walked over. A pool of blood was on the ramp. There'd been a bad accident.

We had a quick way to deplane from the back seat in an F-4, used when we had to piss badly. We slid down the fuselage (preferably after the left engine was shut down), dropped down on the wing, then hopped on the 370-gallon wing tank and dropped a short distance to the ramp. Ralph Caverly did just that.

We all had our own personal side arms in addition to our issued .38 pistols. We carried one gun on our hip, and the second was our "hide out" gun kept in an inside holster concealed by our combat vests. I kept mine loaded with tracers because we had found out our regular pen gun flares wouldn't always penetrate the jungle canopy when we needed to signal rescue helicopters.

We had a wide variety of personal weapons, depending on what you consider a combat weapon. Mine was a customized .45

government model automatic. I had four extra clips on my belt along with the gun. I wasn't anxious to get into a firefight with bad guys using automatic rifles. I figured it was loud and if I was sprinting through the jungle trying to reach a rescue chopper's sling, I could at least get their attention by blasting off a few rounds in their direction.

Ralph for some reason chose a single action .357-magnum revolver, much like guns used by cowboys in the Old West. He unwisely carried a live cartridge under the hammer. When he jumped down on the ramp that day, he jarred the hammer and the pistol fired. The powerful round struck his leg just above the knee and the bullet drove down inside his lower leg into his ankle. Ralph was medivaced to the Philippines for treatment, but his leg was so badly damaged it eventually had to be amputated below the knee. Ralph had flown 168 combat missions and hadn't taken one hit from the enemy.

13 December 66

Dear Lover and now two-year-old Son,

I find it hard to believe that we have fostered a child of two years' growth. It is a shame we don't have another one on the way, as I am sure that our spoiled son could benefit in many ways from having another sister or brother. We should have many nights beside a fireplace in Europe to pursue such things, accompanied by a companionable bottle of wine. N'est-ce pa? At least that is what I hope will result from our trip to Europe. My only misgivings are the grandparents will sorely miss their only grandson. I am afraid I shall find them much older when I return to them next month, which I hope to do.

Enough of such thoughts, however. First I disappointingly did not receive a letter from you today, and even though I realize it is probably our postal system, I am still disappointed, but not heartbroken. I only have thirteen more missions to go, and we received twelve replacements last night to bolster our squadron.

Other news of note. Tragedy struck today. Ralph Caverly shot himself in the leg jumping down from a wing after a mission. A .357 magnum slug and a compound fracture has ended his war, and flying for about nine months. A very unusual accident, and somewhat ironic that he should wound himself after being shot at a full ten months by the enemy. He is expected to fully recover, however.

Christmas approaches and I hope you do not find it too dismal without me. As for myself, I am lucky that I am in a position to ignore it completely, if possible. However, I shall miss you and our son. Our best gift will be a happy reunion early in the year, and this will not fit under any tree or go into a stocking, nor will the love I have for you.

Dad

That afternoon a friend called from the command post. We were tipped off that the brass was coming to confiscate our personal firearms—they were too dangerous for fighter pilots to carry! We took all our personal weapons off the equipment racks and hid them for a few days. No way were we going to lose our extra guns! I can illustrate how strongly we felt about this with an intelligence report from a pilot rescued off the coast of North Vietnam. We read all of these successful rescue reports, looking for tips that would give us an edge and possibly help us stay alive.

This particular pilot ejected during low tide. He deployed his bright orange "Mae West" inflatable water wings and landed in about waist-high water. His flight members circled overhead and called for a rescue chopper. The chopper was off the coast and had four A-1E propeller fighters as escort to lay down fire as the helicopter made its pickup.

His parachute had attracted an armed crowd of North Vietnamese soldiers, who waded out in the tidal flats and captured him. They took his side arm from his hip but missed his sneak gun inside his vest—a small .25–caliber automatic. The enemy soldiers slogged back toward shore with their captive.

The rescue birds, faster than helicopters, arrived first, and the A-1E drivers could see the orange life vest on the downed pilot. They began to strafe in front of him to discourage the Vietnamese from heading to shore. With each strafing pass all but two of the enemy ducked down into the water. Two stayed erect, holding the pilot by the arms. But eventually the bad guys grew anxious taking cover from that barrage of shells. One of the two escorts ducked down in the water at each salvo from the A-1Es. Talk about close shooting! Finally the rescue chopper arrived on the scene.

Timing things just right, during the next strafing run the captive pilot whipped out his little .25 cal and shot his sole standing captor right between the eyes. The second captor popped up from the water. The pilot slugged him and took his rifle. The chopper dropped in fast and rescued the pilot as the A-1Es worked over the area. That little piss-ant gun saved that pilot years of torture and imprisonment.

We would keep our guns. I still have my trusty .45.

Fateful decisions are impossible to understand. One of our guys in a sister squadron got hit over North Vietnam and ejected. When you ejected you went out in the seat, falling strapped into the seat, which trails a small drag chute for stability, until reaching an altitude with enough oxygen. There was a barostat on the seat that automatically released shackles holding the stabilizing chute until you fell below ten thousand feet. This was an automatic feature, just in case the pilot was unconscious. The drag chute then pulled out the main chute and the seat fell away. The pilot descended with only his chute and a survival kit dangling below him.

The guy got out of the plane safely, still sitting in the seat. For some reason he decided to manually separate from it. He pulled the handle that released him. Then he had to reach across his chest with his right arm and pull the D ring held in a metal clip mounted on the left shoulder strap of the parachute harness. He never got a good chute and fell to his death. His body was recovered. Reconstructing his actions, the parachute shop found out that the D ring and metal clip had corroded in the high humidity. That corrosion required more pounds of force pull than Superman could have generated. All of our harnesses were then tested. Ninety percent of them were bad. Sadly, a safety bulletin went out advising us to stay with the seat when ejecting and use the manual system only if we were sure the automatic features did not work.

Another problem pilots had when ejecting was ending up with their chutes caught in the top of a two-hundred-foot-tall tree canopy. The pilot went through the limbs and dangled on the end of the stuck chute. If you could swing in to the trunk you could slither to the ground. If not, you hit the quick releases on the chute harness and free fell two hundred feet to the jungle below. That hurt.

Americans like to solve problems with ingenious devices. This one was solved by placing a compact two-pulley device with a two-hundred-foot nylon line and a mechanical brake in a pouch on the chute harness. This was known as a "tree let-down device." If the chute caught in a tree and you were dangling below, you hooked the looped end of the nylon cord from the device to a metal ring sewn on one chute's riser strap. Then you hit the chute quick release, freeing you from the chute. You were now attached to the top end of the nylon rope. So you released the brake handle but held some tension on it and gently slid down the rope to earth.

John Critzberg was our personal equipment officer. He had jump master parachute training with the Army and was anxious to test out the new equipment. A group of us found a few beers and John, in chute harness, drove us in a van to the base control tower. John climbed up about two flights of steps and found a good place to hook the nylon rope to the tower. He hooked the tree let-down device to his chute harness, stepped off the tower, and swung suspended from the rope.

We all cheered from below. John released the brake, slowly dropping a short distance down the nylon rope. He hit the brake and stopped. We cheered again. John, having quaffed a few beers before his demonstration, laughed. This was fun. He released the brake fully and rapidly dropped down the line. About halfway down he clamped down on the brake lever. The friction heated the nylon line until it melted. The cord broke and John rolled over in midair and fell head first to the ground. He luckily had imbibed enough beer and was hard headed, so he wasn't seriously injured.

We thought it a very fine demonstration. We wrote up a safety bulletin warning not to build up too much speed when descending on the tree let-down device.

I wonder if our test prevented any more accidents.

45. MIG Encounter

We were assigned to escort an EB-66 jamming aircraft, a two-engine converted bomber. Instead of bombs, the bay held six to eight technical guys. They had no windows, just electronic scopes and radar jamming devices. They orbited northwest of Hanoi and tried to jam enemy radar while our strike packages hit a target.

The MIGs, of course, wanted to get them. The EB-66 flew slowly, and our flight of four stupidly flew slowly as well, flying an S pattern behind them at about Mach 0.8. These were faulty tactics, much like the failed bomber escorts the Luftwaffe practiced during the Battle of Britain. I guess our commanders were fans of Hermann Goering's lousy tactics. You had an advantage in aerial combat if you had superior energy to start the battle. Energy equaled speed. Stored energy, altitude. We had given both up to stay level and behind our escort.

I was in Martin's backseat. The raid was on and there was always a lot of radio chatter. I looked up and saw red "golf balls" going over our canopy. A MIG-21 was diving on our group, firing his cannons head on. We hollered "Break!" to the EB-66, punched off our tanks, and lit the afterburners.

The MIG wisely dove straight through. He wouldn't stop to play. We rolled inverted, pulling maximum Gs in the shortest turn possible, accelerating. I found the MIG-21 on radar, eight miles away and separating. End of encounter. We had no weapon to reach the MIG-21 and had to stay with our EB-66. No dogfight today. Just a bunch of guys in the belly of a bomber scared shitless.

Most of the time MIGs preferred not to tangle with F-4s. They liked to go after F-105s carrying heavy bomb loads. Once, coming off a target in the Hanoi area, I was in a flight of four exiting northwest along Thud Ridge. Flights had gotten scrambled up, evading SAMs and ground fire over the target, and flights were calling on the radio trying to get rejoined. Some lone F-105 (Thud) driver spotted two MIGs. He was calling for his wingmen to come help. We heard him and turned towards his position, lit the afterburners, and accelerated.

The two MIGs turned into four. The Thud pilot was excited. He wanted to get some. The four MIGs turned into eight MIGs. The Thud driver had his hands full. We were in full afterburner, pissing fuel out the tail pipe, trying to find him and to even up the odds. As the number of MIGS went up, the Thud driver's voice went up. We could tell he had bitten off more than he could chew. Finally he made a run for it. He came by us at low level going like hell. The F-105 could outrun anything at low level, and he passed under us like were standing still. Never did find those MIGs. A book called *Thud Ridge* by Jack Broughton gives a Thud driver's version of this event.

The afterburner really burned up the fuel. We were low on fuel and had to turn for home. Too bad. It would have been fun to catch eight MIGs all at once. The MIGs had ground radar to assist them and usually picked their spots. If they stayed to fight, we wanted them bad.

I didn't fly on January 2, 1967, when all the F-4 wings led by Robin Olds had a big MIG sweep—code named Bolo. The tactic was using F-105 call signs and flight patterns to deceive the MIGs. On that day they were looking for F-105 bombers. All the MIGs found were F-4s loaded with missiles and guns. Our squadron flew up the east coast of North Vietnam, then into the Hanoi area over a heavy cloud deck. The MIGs that day didn't come up and play with our guys, but our surprise tactics resulted in several MIG kills that day. Someone on that raid has told that story.

46. The "Gift" of Guns

In spite of our superior pilot skills, we weren't doing very well against the MIGs. The enemy had us on their radar and could pick the time and place for their attacks. The usual scenario was to encounter MIGs on the way to a target when we had heavy bomb loads and couldn't maneuver. Then we faced SAMs as we popped up from low altitude to begin our attack on the target and they picked us up on radar. When we dove on a target, we saw a lot of flak. Climbing off the target, scattered by dodging the flak, we had SAMs after us again. Low on fuel by that time, and after SAMs had been fired at us, the MIGs would jump on us once again.

Below 25,000 feet the F-4 could outperform the MIG-21, North Vietnam's best fighter. The F-4 was designed originally for the Navy as a fleet interceptor. Its powerful intercept radar was almost useless for ground mapping. Brilliant minds had determined that dogfighting was passé. Future air combat would rely on technology and missiles.

The F-4 carried four Aim-7 sparrows, radar-guided missiles with up to a thirteen-mile range (head on). It also carried four

Aim-9 sidewinder missiles—heat-seeking, shorter-range missiles. I think they were called sidewinders because they had an erratic pattern guiding towards a target. Who names these things, anyway?

When the infrared seeker head of the sidewinder missile sensed a heat source, a growling tone came over the headset, indicating the missile saw something warm. You could check if your seeker head was good by pointing it at a heat source. Puffy cumulus clouds in the sun excited it.

The Air Force bought the F-4, a big brute of a fighter with lots of power. And it carried a big, varied bomb load. It had no internal gun, but it could carry a twenty-millimeter gun pod on the centerline, mounted below the aircraft.

The C model we flew in Vietnam also didn't have a lead computing gun sight, just a piece of plastic on which a lighted reticule was reflected. We tilted the plastic to make settings for weapons delivery, but other than radar ranging it was a fixed sight, about as good as those used in World War I. Fighters had better, lead computing sights in World War II.

The rules of engagement said we had to visually identify targets as enemy before we could shoot a missile at them. This was a good rule. A lot of friendly aircraft were out there and no one wanted to get shot down by some dumb missile launched by an ally. The problem was that by the time a bogey got close enough to identify visually, we were probably inside minimum range of a sparrow. If we shot then, the missile wouldn't arm. The bogey had probably spotted us, too, and was maneuvering. This meant hard turns and lots of Gs. Under high-G loads we couldn't fire the sidewinders;

they wouldn't come off the airplane right and wouldn't track. The sidewinder was best when we were behind the bogey. A hot exhaust made it go crazy.

What we needed up close, pulling Gs behind some bad guy, was a gun—preferably with a lead computing gun sight. After several MIG engagements and no results, we pleaded with the brass to take off our six-hundred-gallon centerline fuel tank and replace it with the gun pod. They didn't want to give up the fuel so we could stay in the target area longer. But if we had a MIG engagement, we would probably drop our tanks anyway. A clean bird was lighter and maneuvered better. We dropped so many fuel tanks that at times we ran short. We were briefed to keep our tanks, if possible.

I once caused a flight of four to drop their tanks unnecessarily. We were in a high SAM threat area and I caught movement below me out of the corner of my eye. It looked like a white missile coming at us, trailing an exhaust stream. SAMs scared me more than anything else, so I reacted, blew my tanks off, rolled, and broke down into the missile. Eyeballs on it, my brain caught up. The missile was falling, not climbing, and the exhaust was actually fuel streaming from the drop tank.

One of my flight members had a tank that was not feeding. He had punched it off, making no radio call. My buddies saw my tanks go, and my evasive action, so off went their tanks, too. We bobbled around and got reorganized.

On our return, the brass asked why we jettisoned our tanks. "Ask Thrasher" was the reply. I would rather be quick than dead, so I endured the ribbing I received. Anyone can have a bad moment over North Vietnam.

We finally received permission to carry guns. We were now ready to fight just like Spad pilots in World War I, who would drive right up behind the enemy, get real close, and hose him in the ass. The only difference was we had a gun spitting out six thousand rounds a minute. We were also going a little faster.

During the next few weeks our wing shot down five MIGs, all gun kills. Given that success, the 366th became known as the Gunfighters. They're still known by that name and are based at Mountain Home AFB, Idaho.

Later versions of the F-4 had a lead computing gun sight and the E model had a gun built into the nose. Every U.S. fighter built since has an integral gun, in spite of better missiles and radars. Lessons we learned the hard way over North Vietnam.

47. Bullshit Bombs

Believe it or not, the U.S. war arsenal included leaflet bombs—plastic canisters built in two pieces. The fuse fired at a preset altitude, then the canister split open and the leaflets, going five hundred knots, scattered across the countryside. Some civilian decided that if we asked the North Vietnamese to surrender in writing the war would end sooner. He obviously hadn't encountered their determined, intense antiaircraft fire. They remained highly pissed when we bombed them, even with paper.

On my first bullshit bombing mission, at night, I dutifully flew to the target city. Radar-tracking guns gave me a warm reception. That pissed me. No wonder Kissinger had so much trouble at the later peace talks. These people didn't recognize a "peace overture" when they got one "air delivered." One mission providing free toilet paper, yet receiving lots of flak, was enough for me. We should have renamed our Coyote flight call sign Charmin for these bullshit bomb missions.

The next time I got such a mission I flew to the mountains

away from guns, dove into the night, pulled up, and tossed those mothers into the dark. When I landed and debriefed with Intelligence, I told them I laid the bombs right at the "intersection of First and Main Streets" of the intended town. At this point in my Vietnam tour I was wary of wasted missions. I always did my best against real targets, but didn't want to waste my efforts on bullshit missions.

Intelligence guys lived vicariously. Some of them got excited when we debriefed. There was always an intelligence component for every target briefing. Once we had a ho-hum target but a nasty alternate target. Five aircraft had been shot down in the alternate area in the prior week. The Intelligence officer's quote was, "I sure hope you get to go there." What a clown.

Most of us who were later in Germany had completed combat tours in Vietnam. We received an Intelligence briefing about antiaircraft fire from an egghead who'd figured out the radar tracking characteristics of the 57 mm gun. Using a slide rule, he figured that if we jinked (rapidly changed heading and altitude) every 5.632 seconds, or some such silly number, it was impossible for the gun to hit us. We asked him if he had factored in the possibility of multiple guns shooting at us and our running into some of their misses. Never occurred to him.

That system was as poor as the one in North Vietnam, where an Intelligence bird would transmit MIG and SAM warnings, using code words but in the clear over the radio. Nearly all the time we got the SAM warning radio call just after we'd maneuvered away from one and were getting our heart rate back down.

Thank you, Lord, for giving me 20/10 vision. I can still spot ducks way ahead of my buddies in the duck blind. That is one reason why I'm here to tell this story. The other must have been fate.

48. Crazy Engine

I was flying blue four on a target in North Vietnam, over which was a good deal of flak. We bombed and jinked around, engines at full throttle, avoiding flak concentrations. Getting scattered in the process, we rejoined and headed for home.

Back at altitude, about thirty thousand feet, my lead throttled back to 98 percent, giving his wingmen about 2 percent power to maneuver with. Tail-end Charlie, I was the last guy to throttle back. As I did, the RPM gauge on one engine went *down* and the other sped *up* over 100 percent. What in the hell was going on? I pushed both throttles up. One RPM gauge went *up* and the other *down*; both engines went to 100 percent. My first thought was that one of my throttles had been hooked up backwards. No, that couldn't be true. How could I have taken off with a big bomb load, both throttles worked full forward in afterburner?

I pulled back both throttles again. Same result. I instantly knew what the problem was. Eyelids at the back of the engine control the exhaust nozzle, and a throttle position sensor tells the nozzles to close to increase exhaust speed when full throttle is selected. When I pulled the throttle back on the bad engine, the nozzles opened, reducing back pressure on the turbine. The bad engine sped off to the races. Jet engines turn at several thousand RPMs. When you over-speed the engine, bad things happen.

I had an engine fuel control computer to prevent this from happening. Mine malfunctioned. The bad engine began to rumble. I either had to shut that engine down or have turbine blades fly off and cause real damage. I shut down the engine and began to lag behind my flight.

I called lead. "Give me two," I said, which meant 2 percent—I needed a little help keeping up. That wasn't enough, so I asked for two more.

"What's up?" asked lead.

"I lost an engine."

It was a long, long trip home. I kept my eyeballs glued to my remaining engine, watching for the telltale wiggle of gauges that would indicate trouble. I even took my helmet off once to listen for what I imagined were strange engine noises. It seemed to take forever to get out of North Vietnam, and I was really glad the F-4 had two engines.

49. Crew Chiefs

Crew chiefs were young guys like us. We had specific tail numbers assigned to us. Both our name and our crew chief's were painted on the side of the plane. Chiefs worked ten- to twelve-hour days, seven days a week, taking great pride in their work. We trusted them to give us sound aircraft to fly into combat and were seldom disappointed.

While we were on a mission, they waited and met us in the refueling pits on our arrival. When their bird didn't return they were crestfallen, wondering if a malfunction had jeopardized the aircrew. I saw some break down in tears when a flight returned without their bird. Our commander, Felix Fowler, decided our crew chiefs deserved a ride in their bird if it went up on a test hop. He let them have rides in the backseat on unarmed test hops over the sea. The chiefs didn't have altitude chamber training or a host of other official requirements to fly. They just loved their birds. Felix didn't let paperwork or regulations get in his way.

A test hop with a clean bird was a blast. We took off, keeping the engines in full afterburner, and zoomed to 45,000 feet in about two minutes. Then, afterburners going, we bunted the nose down, reducing the angle of attack on the wing, decreasing drag, and made a run over Mach 2. It became a contest among the crew chiefs as to who had the fastest F-4. Bets were made. Some crew chiefs even waxed their bird, hoping vainly that would help its speed.

Over Mach 2, airspeed built gradually. On a Mach run we went out to sea like a bat out of hell for over one hundred miles. We watched two things: the airspeed indicator and the fuel gauge. Near the end of a Mach run, airspeed crept up as the fuel gauge plummeted. We pilots wanted our crew chiefs to win the speed contest, but also wanted to get back home. Most of us came back on fumes.

Talk about happy! One nineteen-year-old winner enjoyed the ride of his life, plus won booze and bucks from his buddies.

A squadron commander has the responsibility for the pilots and crew chiefs and other maintenance people, about three hundred total. Felix wasn't afraid of younger, higher ranking officers. More than once we saw him tell a full colonel lacking his combat experience, "Colonel, that is the dumbest thing I have ever heard." Ranking officers found that hard to take, but Felix was a big man, about six feet four and 230 pounds. He stared them down and watched them squirm. He had allowed four young lieutenants to upgrade to aircraft commander, and the youngsters in our sister squadrons were jealous.

Felix took care of his enlisted troops. Believe it or not, we ran out of beer at Danang. First there was no domestic beer, then only Korean beer, and finally only Vietnamese beer. The Vietnamese beer was called *bam mi ba* (thirty-three). We believed it was brewed with formaldehyde. It was bitter and two or more gave you a headache. Fighting a war without beer was unjust, so Felix took up a collection among the pilots to buy beer in the Philippines. He cut bogus orders for two of our guys to go and buy a few pallets.

Our guys, without real orders, hitched a ride on a transport as crew members. Once there they purchased the beer, then spent time on the ramp at Clark Field trying to hitch a ride back. A lot of transports had room for extra crew, but no room for the pallets of beer. Finally they found a general's C-54 transport going to Danang. The pilot had to get the OK from the general to load the beer. He got a go, and our boys and the beer headed for Danang. Inbound, our two beer guys got on the squadron radio frequency to announce the beer was en route. Word spread throughout the squadron, especially to our crew chiefs.

As is customary for a general, staff cars and brass greeted him on landing. He had a much bigger welcoming party in the vans and trucks behind his plane, who were offloading the beer. Somewhere our maintenance troops had found an old horse tank (maybe left over from the French) and filled it with ice and beer. That night the 389th had a hangar party. The rest of the wing was green with envy.

Felix was an inveterate smoker, too. One night when I joined up on him I thought he had a fire in the cockpit, as the canopy lit up soon after take-off. Felix had his oxygen mask off and had just lit up a cigarette.

We were given ration cards that allowed us to buy five fifths of booze a month. Not having ice made drinking whisky tough for young lieutenants. Several of our older sergeants were not bothered by the lack of ice and would use up their ration cards before month's end. That's when they would borrow a card from one of their pilots. Felix had taught us well.

There's been talk of drug problems in Vietnam. We had no problems with our crew chiefs or maintenance guys. They had pride and kept busy keeping us flying. We had complete trust in them. Most of the problems in the Air Force were with support troops with too much time on their hands and no mission identity.

Felix knew how to motivate. We had good records for aircraft availability and mission success. He was promoted to lieutenant colonel, to the chagrin of a few wise guys above him. Men with good leaders can do great things. There is a big difference between managing and leading.

50. Christmas at Danang

On Christmas Eve I flew another night mission. It was rainy and foggy. After the mission I decided to go to midnight church services. In my poncho, I walked along the perimeter to the church, alone in the gloom. The night was eerie, and my thoughts were black as well. As usual, flares were going off, incoming and outgoing fire. I wondered if I might need to use my .45 if some guys in black pajamas decided to sneak through the perimeter fence and hit the troops gathered in the church.

I had a lot going through my mind that night. How could I be celebrating this Christian event after bombing people who were not? How were they different than me? Could anyone or anything justify killing another human being?

I opened the doors and found the church packed with Marines, Army, and Air Force all wet in ponchos, some in helmets and battle gear. The blunt odor of sweat, mold, and grime permeated the air of the church entryway.

I was late, but caught the last of the sermon. The chaplain did his best to tell us we were doing God's work, serving our country. I wondered what our "heathen" enemy felt they were doing? The sermon took me back to the moment of my worst crisis of conscience in Vietnam.

A few months before I'd been carrying napalm on a dawn flight, assigned to put some preventive fire around a special-forces camp on a Sunday morning. No bad guys were known to be there. We were just keeping the enemy alert, and hopefully helping the Green Beret's morale. Four of us dropped our napalm by the camp as directed on the radio. I had one napalm canister that didn't release, so I carried it home, hoping it wouldn't come off upon landing.

On the way back we got a radio call, directing us to a FAC. A group of Vietcong had attacked a South Vietnamese outpost at dawn. The guerillas had retreated and a FAC had gone airborne at daybreak to look for them. He had spotted them carrying their wounded and resting by a well a few miles from their attack. We still had 20 mm ammo, so the FAC fired his smoke rocket and we attacked. We strafed. The enemy ran. It was shoot, run, shoot, run, over some distance. Finally the survivors took refuge in a fairly substantial building. We strafed. The FAC asked if we had any heavier ordnance.

I had the lone napalm can. If I could use an alternate release system, I might be able to drop it. So in I came. Adrenaline flowed and the dragon in me again took over. We had been killing the bad guys. I wanted to finish the job. I made a direct hit on that building, blowing it up completely. The FAC gave me a "job well done." We climbed out with several KIA [killed in action] confirmed.

As I headed home I wondered if there'd been a family in there having a quiet Sunday morning when all of a sudden bad guys broke in with the sheriff after them. I felt terrible. It wrenched my gut for several days. It still bothers me. Since Vietnam I have been a pretty mild-mannered guy. Assholes don't usually upset me. Some friends say I'm too easygoing. I think I'm afraid to let my dragon out again.

Killing people is bad work. You can't paint it any other way. I resolved then never again to let anyone categorize right or wrong for me. I also decided never to be in a fight unless the stakes were very high.

That night generated lots of thoughts of home, and questions about morality and my duty. It was the worst Christmas of my life.

51. Carols at the "Doom Club"

We stood down on Christmas Day for yet another truce, so a lot of guys were at the Doom Club. Most were in a lousy mood. As usual, it was humid and rainy and we were miserable, missing our families and homes. To cheer us up the USO had brought in entertainment that evening. Some Australian girl was to sing Christmas carols.

It was standing room only, with about six feet separating the singer from the audience. She was surrounded. For accompaniment, the singer had a male assistant with a tape recorder. She started to sing. The electricity system was fifty cycle current, not sixty. As a result, the tape recorder played slower than normal. The singer would get ahead of the music and pause to get back on track. It was terrible.

We were in an awful Christmas mood, some very drunk. After the second pause, someone shouted "Take it off," trying to turn the singer into a stripper. That chorus grew at each subsequent pause. She was upset. Some of the guys were upset she wouldn't strip. She got really nervous, with guys packed in the room, just a few feet from her. Eventually she quit in tears and was rushed into the club manager's office. He was a new second lieutenant and scared, too. He locked the door.

The woman really was safe, although I'm sure she felt threatened by a rough-mouthed group of men closely surrounding her. It was an abysmal end to a joyless holiday. We all left the club, walked through the rain, and crawled under our mosquito nets in our un-air-conditioned barracks to try to sleep and dream of home.

Christmas Day 1966

Dear Hon and Son,

Well, we did not have a white Christmas in Danang, but it was plenty wet. We really had a monsoon last night. Water was ankle deep all the way across the street. We had a steak fry for the whole squadron, with a hundred cases of beer.

There was a singer at the club and she had a bad time. All of her background music was recorded and it did not work out too well. She ended up her act with some Christmas songs and everyone was supposed to sing along but it was not too successful. With the downpour and being here for Christmas, not many were in the mood for Christmas songs.

The sun came out this morning and I went to church, and then had a big turkey dinner at the club. It was pretty good too. It is three p.m. now and I am looking for something to kill the afternoon. Tomorrow, the war begins for another week, then two more days of peace, and by then I should be ready to come home. I only have six more to go now.

I am packing a footlocker for home, and another for Germany. When the time comes, I am going to be ready to leave instantaneously, on ten minutes' notice. That is how much I want to come home and see you both. I hope your Christmas was as good as could be, and I want to thank you for the card. It makes me feel good. I am sorry all I had to give you was the promise that I will be home to you soon.

We are very lucky this Christmas, even if we are apart. Ralph Caverly had his foot amputated, and may lose the rest of his leg. That is really tough news. Last night a civilian air cargo carrier crashed a mile and a half short of the runway and over one hundred twenty Vietnamese were killed, and many injured. So we really do have things to be thankful for this Christmas. So, do not feel too sorry for us. I love you and will be home soon.

Love, Dad

52. Milk, Ice Cream, and Hot Pants

There are things we all missed from home. Hometown girls (with round eyes) were scarce except for nurses, but there were things we missed more.

Civilian airliners on contract to the military used our ramp and parked near our refueling pits. We learned that they had milk and ice cream on board. When one landed, four to eight armed pilots, just back from a combat mission, raced up the jet's stairs. The stewardesses were initially shaken by the invasion (this was before airline hijacking became popular) but didn't have to fear for their virtue. When we raided the pantry they relaxed. The only goodies we wanted were cartons of fresh milk and ice cream. I believe we would have taken them at gunpoint, if necessary. Word was passed among the airline crews, and future flights arrived with a lot of extras.

The USO sent entertainers. I flew over the Bob Hope show around Christmas Day and saw a lot of Marines on that hillside. One day two "babes" from television and their cigar-smoking manager visited our squadron. They, of course, drew a crowd. They wore hot pants, see-through plastic raincoats, and white go-go boots. It was the '60s! We asked what they did and they mentioned a TV show we had never heard of.

Being officers and gentlemen, we politely offered them coffee. Our building had no running water, just the tanker outside. As a result we seldom washed anything. (But our coffee was lethal even without extra germs.) It didn't go over well at all. They politely accepted the gross cups but didn't touch a drop.

Some of our pilots, wearing combat vests, guns, and flight gear, ready to go on a mission, were standing in front of a painting of an F-4 taking off with a full bomb load. A babe asked, "What do you boys do?"

"We kill people," one answered.

I guess you need boobs, not brains, to be on a TV show. Nice boobs, though.

53. Crazed Base Commander

As strange as war in the air over North Vietnam was, even stranger things could happen on the ground when staff pukes got carried away with their positions. I would not have believed this next story if I had not been a participant in the fiasco.

In an Air Force wing, the wing commander is the boss. Squadron commanders report up to him and all the pilots and guys working on the aircraft are in that chain of command. The base commander is in charge of housekeeping, administration, supply, and air police. He also reports to the wing commander. Pilots do not report to him. In some cases the guy is not even a pilot.

At Danang, we got a new base commander who was going to run the place like a Stateside base. Soon we were getting tickets for dirty trucks on our way to the flight line. Never mind the fact that the roads were rutted and muddy and we got thirty inches of rain a month.

We returned from one night's last Coyote flight about 0700 and headed to the Doom Club for some drinks. The bar was closed and a strap padlocked the beer cooler. Evidently our drinking in the early morning upset those going to office work. We lifted the strap, slid open the cooler, and took some beers, careful to leave the proper payment on the cooler.

The next morning we found the cooler locked again, this time with a padlock on each handle so we couldn't lift the strap and open it. We were in the 366th wing. We fighter pilots knew most staff pukes weren't too bright, so combination 3660 or 0366 worked. We had beer again. Never underestimate a fighter pilot's ability to get post-mission booze.

The night squadrons protested the bar closing. Someone with some brains heard our pleas. The bar remained open.

We often flew Ranch Hand escort. These were C-123s equipped to spray Agent Orange and defoliate the jungle. We didn't know what the stuff really was, but knew it was bad because you saw the vegetation change color soon after it was sprayed.

The Vietnamese hated the Ranch Hands. They were unarmed, flew slow, and took lots of ground fire, so they wore helmets and flak jackets. When they reported ground fire, we dropped bombs to make them feel better, probably not doing much harm to the enemy. We had a lot of respect for these guys. One of their navigators took a hit to the helmet. The round entered on one side and bounced all the way around his head, bouncing off the inside of his helmet along the way. He had some deep gouges in his head but wasn't wounded seriously. Although when is a head wound not serious? When he was released from the hospital, head swathed in bandages, we had a welcome back party. The gong rang and drinks were on the house. It was a good party.

Soon a group was firing beer cans up into the overhead fans. Empty ones were light auto weapons. Full ones were heavy antiaircraft fire. Just as the party was going strong, in came the new base commander, accompanied by three nervous air policemen with M-16s. He was going to arrest all of us. Wiser heads prevailed.

Next there appeared "One-Way Street" signs on our only road in the compound, and then a "No Parking" sign in front of the Doom Club. Since it rained all the time it would be wet and damn inconvenient to not park at the club. We backed our truck over the sign, parked, and went in. Early the next morning we were geared up to fly north. Felix Fowler, now a lieutenant colonel, finished our mission briefing. The new base commander, a full colonel, asked to speak to the troops.

"Men," he said, "we know you've been taking down the 'No Parking' signs. I'm here to tell you the next guys that do will have their medals taken away and be sent home."

We were too stunned for words. So . . . if I leave the sign up I get to go to North Vietnam and get shot. If I take it down, I go home. This crazy guy thought this was punishment. Several of us made a pact. Those returning from the mission *will take down the sign*. We were mad as hell. Look out, North Vietnam!

Returning safely, we drove our crew van to the Doom Club and looked for the "No Parking" sign. The base commander had his engineers bolt the sign high up on the building. Our "mission" required new tactics. We drove to our engine shop, got some bolt cutters from our maintenance crew, drove back to the Doom Club, and parked in front. In we went for a meal and some drinks. Then it was time to launch our offensive.

Four of us in ponchos stepped into the rain. Since we were on a mission, we all carried side arms. We noticed an air policeman across the street, backed under the eave of a building, rain dripping on his helmet and poncho. There was a second one next to the adjacent building, also trying to stay dry. This could be trouble. We emptied our plastic billfolds and pooled our scrip. (We were paid in monopoly money so greenbacks would not leave the U.S., and we carried plastic map holders for billfolds because leather got moldy). I took half the money and approached the air policeman across the street.

"Good evening," I said.

"Good evening, sir," he replied.

"What are you doing, airman?"

"Guarding, sir."

"Are you guarding the signs?"

"Yes, sir."

I told him we were going to take the signs, and that we'd already been shot at today so once more would be nothing new, but we would shoot back. I showed him my side arm under my poncho and gave him the money for the trouble he'd have when the signs were gone. Then I asked, "You're not going to shoot, are you?"

"No, sir, I will not."

"Thanks."

We loaded up the crew van, backed it to the Doom Club, climbed on top, and cut the bolts holding the sign. We put it into the van and sped into the rainy night.

Danang was under attack almost every night and our crazy base commander took two guys off perimeter defense to guard signs. This guy was the enemy.

Fortunately, wise heads prevailed and the crazy commander disappeared quietly from Danang.

And that is why we respected our enemy but despised staff pukes.

54. Strange Bridges

The night before a mission, squadrons received "frag orders" outlining the target, number of aircraft, and ordnance. We reviewed them, assigned crew and aircraft, and planned the mission. This time our frag target was an underwater bridge in Laos. We often had strange targets.

The Ho Chi Minh trail ran down through Laos into South Vietnam. We spent a lot of effort trying to interdict movement there. The target photos showed that the enemy had built a bridge underwater to hide it. We could see its outline under the water.

The 7th Air Force headquarters' weapon of choice, napalm, amused us. Did they expect us to boil it to death? We called to ask if they were serious and they said they'd get back to us. Someone with brains must have been on the job because the next day we were loaded with bombs.

Every twenty missions in North Vietnam took a month off a pilot's one-year tour. If you reached a hundred you rotated home, no matter how many months it took. I was close to going home.

All I needed to do was get to my forty-mission count over North Vietnam. I had orders cut to return home in January. Each "counter" was a step closer. I ended up with forty missions over the North, 187 in the South and Laos, and one that the International Control Commission counted as Cambodia. I was really happy to take on this next target bridge.

Our target was the last standing bridge on Route One, not far above the DMZ and close to the coast. All of the other bridges on Route One had been bombed out several times, and the North Vietnamese had built bypasses around each more than once. North Vietnamese bulldozer operators had job security.

Bridges were hard targets to knock out with dumb bombs. You generally had to attack on a diagonal to the bridge axis and try to hit just short of the intended target and walk your string of bombs through the bridge. The bombs come off in a timed ripple release, so they hit several meters apart. It took lots of bombs and sorties to knock a single bridge out.

We youngsters were not unhappy to get this target. Although it was of little value, it was relatively safe. First, it was barely in North Vietnam. Second, it was close to the sea, so we would be off the target and away from guns quickly. Third, there was no reason to defend the bridge, so no flak was expected. This mission counted the same as eating flak, SAMs, and MIGs over Hanoi. We appreciated the easy ones.

Our wing operations officer, a full colonel, occasionally flew with us. He was old (way over forty) and had to wear glasses to read his checklist. Being a smart guy, he decided we would concentrate our bombs in a tight four-ship formation. (He wanted to look good to headquarters.) Usually we rolled in individually, set up our own sight picture, and bombed on our own. But lieutenants didn't argue with colonels, so we agreed that it would be a brilliant tactic.

Up to the target area we flew. We saw bridges and more bridges, many less than a mile apart. The colonel orbited and orbited, looking for the one not yet bombed out. The area looked like the moon—bomb craters everywhere. It was hard to see our target, unless you had young eyes. All of us youngsters spotted the right bridge, but we had to tuck in close to our leader to follow his tactics.

The colonel was over the wrong bridge and about to bomb the one just *south* of our intended target. But down we went, and when we saw his bombs release, we all pickled. Bombs away! We pulled out of the dive and turned to look behind. We saw dirt, water, and smoke in a giant plume from the explosions. Our salvo obscured the bridge.

Back at base, we debriefed the mission. The colonel was certain we'd destroyed the bridge. We could only agree heartily.

That night we got the reconnaissance photos. The target bridge still stood. There were so many bomb craters around no one could tell which were ours. Never fear, we got the same target the next day.

Again we flew, this time in an even tighter formation, concentrating our firepower. It was the same tale, but a different chapter. The colonel circled our flight, young lieutenants' eyes again spotting the intended target, but we maintained radio discipline and tightened up on the colonel's wing. The colonel seemed unsure. He maneuvered and rolled in, this time bombing the bridge just *north* of our intended target. We dropped. More bomb craters.

We loved it. No shots fired. The entire mission took about half an hour. Two counters. Eighteen more would knock a month off our tour. We lieutenants would do this for the rest of the war.

Again, the battle damage photos came in. The bridge stood. The colonel was dumbfounded. We assured him that we would get it next time, and that we were anxious to go again. An easy counter. But mercifully for the colonel, the target was pulled. The bridge would stand. Our commander was disappointed. We were, too. We were happy to attack this cream puff target every day until we had our magic forty.

55. Replacements

We were counting on going home in January 1967. In December 1966 our replacements were arriving, and we had to train them. Our job was to fly in their backseats as they flew the wing position with our veteran flight leaders.

We flew nights. One of the new guys was briefing a new lieutenant. They were going up to Dong Hoi, which had some good gunners. Those of us not flying casually listened to the briefing. Our guy told the new lieutenant that he wanted to draw the guns out so he could hit them. He told him to turn his navigation lights on so they would shoot, then flight lead, at a lower altitude, would swoop in with napalm and attack the guns.

We were amused. No one ever turned navigation lights on, not even in the pattern around Danang, much less North Vietnam. Charlie still shot at you on final approach here. Transport pilots found that out as they came in from the States with lights on. But the lieutenant didn't know any better, so he followed the plan.

He turned on his lights and the gunners cut loose. But our

fearless leader had miscalculated. He was between the gun positions and his gullible wingman. The gunners didn't know he was around but scored a direct hit. He turned east, on fire, and headed for the sea. The crew bailed out just before the plane exploded and was rescued by an amphibian. Our wet, shaken, but unhurt warriors arrived at the Doom Club for stiff drinks. The new guy learned his lesson and we lost our sixth aircraft, one-third of the planes we flew across the Pacific nine months earlier.

As we trained our replacements, I got the assignment of flying in the backseat of the new squadron operations officer, a lieutenant colonel who would be number two in command of the squadron. We, too, went to Dong Hoi. We flared the barge crossing, the guns lit up, and behold—we actually caught barges out on the river. This was a rare treat. So often we lit up the crossings and found nothing.

This new guy couldn't see the barges. I was pounding on the canopy yelling and trying to point them out from the backseat. My new guy just wouldn't put the nose of the airplane down into the eerily lit target with tracers coming up, no matter how I tried to coach him. He turned out to sea. We ended up jettisoning our bombs over the water. With new guys like this, it would be a long war.

On our landing approach, this rookie (who had previously flown a desk and never a fighter before the F-4) dropped speed. I watched the angle of attack indicators in back and could tell we were way too slow. Our nose was too high. Fearing for my life I hit both throttles before landing. We hit hard and scraped the stabilator tail on the runway.

The next night I drew the same guy. We bombed ineffectively, and on approach he got slow again. I hit the throttles again. After debriefing I went to our operations officer, Colonel Hawkins, and told him I wouldn't fly with this new guy again. Here I was, about to come home after over two hundred combat missions, and this guy was trying to get me killed. Hawkins took care of me.

Soon I had other worries—that a Christmas truce might slow down my progress towards getting my forty counters.

16 December 66

Darling,

Got rained out of a counter today, but the magic number is now eleven. The weather is going to have to help a little if I am going to get home early. We are also having to check out our replacements, and might lose a few counters that way.

I want you to look again for that USAA insurance information. I am also going to write my sponsor Monday, and then his wife will get your address. You are right about the mass of red tape involved. I get tired just thinking about it.

I do not think I am going to get away anywhere until I leave. I don't want to go anywhere until I get my counters. Right now I am worrying that the truce might be extended and then I will be stuck over here all that much longer. Keep your fingers crossed for good weather, no extension of the truce, and bad aim for the NVN gunners.

Well, it is two hours later, and I still have not thought of anything good to write, so I guess I will take a break and play some cribbage with Sloan. Well, just beat him two straight games, and he is going to sulk in bed.

We are supposed to be under a high threat of a mortar attack this week, according to intelligence, but the worst thing around here at night seems to be the bugs. I believe I have acquired some bed bugs. Every night I wake up with bites all over me, even though I sleep under a mosquito net. They usually feed on the back of my hands for some reason. Tonight I sprayed the bottom of my mattress with bug spray, so they will either all be on top or else I will have killed them. Since it is late I think I will close. You know I love you honey—fat, wrinkles, and all. My one thought is coming home to you. Soon too, I hope.

Dad

56. Shortest Mission

At Danang there was so much outgoing mortar and artillery fire from the Marines that we were given safe flight corridors below twenty thousand feet. We were supposed to fly out and return through these headings to avoid our own ground fire. One of our new crews got scrambled at night on a close air support mission. Eager to get to the fight, they turned right after getting airborne. Down they went, ejecting less than a mile off the end of the runway.

They landed in a ditch, staying there all night while the Marines and the enemy shot at each other over the top of them. Each clutched his personal side arm and hoped that the next guy to jump in the ditch was a friendly. When daylight came the bad guys, as usual. returned home. The Marines went out and brought our guys back.

Every aircraft loss required an investigation. A team of three pilots was assigned the duty of examining the crash scene, about a half-mile off the end of the runway. Two enemy rifle rounds through the windshield of their four-wheel-drive pickup concluded the investigation. Enemy fire was listed as the cause of aircraft loss.

We later studied maps of the base and figured that our guys overflew an active Marine mortar position. Our conclusion was the Marines shot the plane down.

Combat flight log: thirty seconds. Surely this was the shortest combat flight of the war in which to have been shot down, even by friendlies.

We had now lost seven aircraft: three shot down by the enemy, three lost to accidents, and one shot down by the Marines. It was our final loss.

57. Going Home

In anticipation of my return, Carole had expressed some fears that I may not be the same person I once was. The war had certainly changed me, but I tried to reassure her that we'd be fine.

2 January 67

Well, I still have only one more mission to go, but I still do not have any idea as to when I will be getting home. We were all put in for port call the tenth of this month, but one of the wheels in the wing said we are to stay until the end of the month, and for those of us with thirty-nine missions to not fly another counter until then. We have enough replacements to leave. As a matter of fact, this building is getting crowded. Needless to say, we really are not too happy right now. I don't know what the final result will be, but I hope to hell I get out of here soon. It is really bad allowing the anxiety to build up about this last mission, and believe me, the longer I sit around and wait, the longer and tighter my gut gets. If I could just fly it and get it over, it won't be any problem, I am sure.

Thanks so much for the long letter. I had not received one for three days and was almost convinced that you had stopped writing me already. I need to know that you love me and I have two wonderful people to come home to, and begin to have a normal life again. I am really sick of all the muck and rain and semi-existence.

I loved your long letter and discussion of what I thought could turn into a problem. You are quite right about my being ignorant and even gross on occasion, but I hope you will never be afraid to talk to me about anything. Nothing makes me feel worse than ever knowing that you have some kind of fears about me. You see, I really love you, and I realize it more than ever now. I guess I do not express it right or am not ever aware of it enough when I am home.

I too missed buying you some goofy presents and sharing Christmas with our boy. Speaking of church, you and I are going together when I get home.

You know, as I think of coming home for real, I still feel I have changed, and our marriage will not be the same as our first three years. I am sure it will be better, however. You are right, we are almost still strangers, but I think if we get along so well as strangers, we certainly will do better. I love your funny nose, and hope I can write you and definitely say I will be home soon to love you up good.

Dad

My final mission was memorable only because it was my last over North Vietnam. It was now mid January 1967, and seventeen from our squadron were headed home at the same time. All of us were assigned to bases in Germany as our next post. We completed our missions and the obligatory celebration at the Doom Club.

The next morning, hung over, we were loaded on a transport to Saigon for out-processing. This procedure, which should take about one hour, was a three-day ordeal. Each day we stood around in lines filling out forms and waiting for a flight assignment. Each night we were bussed into Saigon to stay at a hotel that looked like a big, dark, stone haunted house. No electricity. The whole hotel was a cavern. A wire mesh screen hung out front to keep grenades and satchel charges from being thrown in.

Our guards were two Vietnamese "white mice." They looked about twelve years old and afraid. I was certain if any bad guys showed up they'd Di-di (run).

I thought I was a target. I was unarmed. It was hard to sleep. I had made it through 228 combat missions and now I had to worry that some sneaky son of a bitch would blow up our hotel. This really was a stupid war.

As we out-processed, we were assembled into groups that would fill 707 airliners. We soon got to recognize members of our group. One guy was an Air Force sergeant who showed up each day drunk and hung over. He was a noncombatant but obviously had a problem.

On day three we finally boarded the airliner and took our time machine to Guam, leaving the world of combat and rapidly being transported to the real world.

Many years later I went to see the movie *The Deer Hunter*, starring Robert De Niro. It showed a going-away celebration at a local bar in Pennsylvania, then cut to mortar rounds going off in a field in Vietnam. That quick transition, plus the street scenes, were very real to me and captured the concept of the time machine. As the movie transported me back to Vietnam, I felt long-suppressed emotions building within me. I almost had to walk out of the theater.

The only other movie that generated such emotion was *Saving Private Ryan*. In the graphic opening scenes of the Normandy landings, our troops finally broke out from the beach. As they stormed enemy bunkers and overran them, our soldiers shot several Germans trying to surrender. For me that movie captured the fear and adrenaline that helps a soldier survive and frees his inner dragon. It clearly depicted the priorities found in combat: One, stay alive; two, save your buddies; three, accomplish the mission. It showed the dragon inside a combatant, which emerges when adrenaline overcomes intellect. That dragon still has me wary of him.

At Guam we got a break while the airliner refueled. Our sergeant was still drunk. He must have had a stash of booze somewhere.

Our next stop was Travis AFB outside of San Francisco. Most of the returning pilots phoned ahead to get airline reservations to their hometowns. We were anxious to be home. We had a tight schedule to make some flights. Not wanting to waste a minute, we planned to take taxicabs to the civilian airport.

We landed at Travis and were assembled in a room for final out-processing. We wanted to get going. When our drunken sergeant passed out, the local health officials who were clearing us back into the world became concerned. Would we be exposing the States to plague, Dengue fever, malaria, or other tropical diseases? The health department decided to quarantine us. To no avail we tried to convince them that the guy was just a drunk. But our health official in white hat and uniform, armed with clipboard, was firmly in charge. None of us could leave the room until he cleared us.

I found several Marines in the latrine plotting to kill the guy with a KA-BAR knife and make a run for freedom. As an officer and a gentleman, I convinced them this would only add to the time it would already take us to get home.

The health department guy was oblivious that over one hundred pissed-off combatants surrounded him. Some of them had been killing people for a year and would not have minded one more KIA.

Telephone calls to higher authorities were made. We were each given cards to carry in our wallets that stated if we were found unconscious we may have the plague or the disease of the month. After an eternity we were released. The cards given us littered the ground outside the building as we rushed to find cabs. Many of us had missed our connections, rescheduled, and waited.

The real world was amazing. I went to an airport barbershop and asked for a shave. The barber asked if he could use a safety razor, as he didn't give many shaves. At least I didn't have to worry about him cutting my throat.

We found a bar. A curvy, round-eyed waitress in mesh stockings and a brief barmaid outfit took my drink order, a martini. She returned with it. I gave her a dollar and told her to keep the change. She curtly informed me the drink was $1.50. My drinks had been ten or fifteen cents the past year. Welcome back.

We hung out in the bar, giving each comrade a raucous farewell, escorting each warrior to his gate as he finally headed home. Our ranks slowly thinned, and my flight finally arrived. I flew through Denver, arriving in Omaha after midnight.

Carole, Brad, Carole's mother, Edna, and her father, Rudy, were there to meet me. I gave my wife and son the biggest hug in the world and Carole and I had a long kiss. God, I had missed them. God, it felt great to finally be home. Carole literally tossed Brad into her parents' arms and took me by the hand. She had reserved a room at the Blackstone Hotel, where we'd spent our wedding night. This night was even better.

Fate prevailed. I was home at last.

ACKNOWLEDGEMENTS

When you write a book, the process takes on a life of its own. A lot of nurturing is needed for a first-time author. I received much help and encouragement in telling this story. First, my loving wife, Carole, urged me to get started and saved the letters that helped so much in recapturing my thoughts and emotions. I received tremendous support in my writing from my ex-sister-in-law, Paula Iacampo, who knows the literary world. I was amazed when best-selling author Stephen Mansfield called after reading the manuscript she'd sent him and told me the story was compelling and well written. His encouragement kept me going forward. My close friend and business partner, Bob Suddick, kept these stories alive as he listened patiently to some of these stories on long rides to Kansas for over thirty years.

Fighter pilots like to be in control. I worried about turning my memoir, especially the letters home, over to an editor. I found two: Karen Davis and Sheryl Trittin. They took my story and shaped into good writing. Thanks for the help.

My former comrades in arms were a blessing. They shared some laughs and tears, helped my faulty memory, and added their thoughts, not to mention their own contributions. They are Murray Sloan, Gene Quick, Larry Day, Bob Winegar, Fred Frostic, Bob Wickman, and Ed Montgomery. Thanks for your service, comradeship, and friendship. This is your story, too.

ABOUT THE AUTHOR

Gary Thrasher served seven years in the U.S. Air Force, following his combat tour in Vietnam with a three-and-a-half-year tour in Germany. He left the Air Force in 1970, returned to Nebraska with his family that grew to include six boys, and started a career in banking. He became the chief operating officer of Nebraska's largest bank, then CEO of a major label printing company in Omaha. He remains active in banking as chairman of a Kansas bank holding company. He and his wife, Carole, divide their time between homes in Bellevue, Nebraska, and Tubac, Arizona, and a hunting cabin on an island on the Platte River.

Contact Gary at Gthrasher@me.com

For more on 389/366th go to Phantom Letters.net